# Diana, The Making of a Media Saint

# Diana,
# The Making
# of a Media Saint

*Edited by*
Jeffrey Richards,
Scott Wilson &
Linda Woodhead

.

I.B.Tauris *Publishers*
LONDON ● NEW YORK

Published in 1999 by I.B.Tauris & Co Ltd
Victoria House, Bloomsbury Square, London WC1B 4DZ
175 Fifth Avenue, New York NY 10010
Website: http:// www.ibtauris.com

In the United States and Canada distributed by St Martin's Press
175 Fifth Avenue, New York NY 10010

ISBN 1 86064 388 4

A full CIP record for this book is available from the British Library
A full CIP record for this book is available from the Library of Congress

Library of Congress catalog card: available

Typeset by The Midlands Book Typesetting Company, Loughborough
Printed and bound in Great Britain by WBC Ltd, Bridgend

# Contents

# Contributors

Rosalind Brunt is a Research Fellow in Media Studies at Sheffield Hallam University.

Alvin Cohan is Senior Lecturer in Politics at Lancaster University.

Simon Critchley is Director of Theoretical Studies at the University of Essex.

Richard Fenn is Professor of Christianity and Society at Princeton Theological Seminary.

Paul Heelas is Professor in Religion and Modernity at Lancaster University.

Emily Lomax is completing a PhD on contemporary British Asian literature in the Department of English, Lancaster University.

Jeffrey Richards is Professor of Cultural History at Lancaster University

Scott Wilson is Senior Lecturer in English at Lancaster University.

Linda Woodhead is Lecturer in Christian Studies at Lancaster University

# Introduction: Saint Diana

*Aprés ma mort, je ferai tomber une pluie de roses*
*(After my death, I will make roses fall like rain)*
Motto on a statue of Saint Teresa of Jesus, Paris[1]

Diana was no saint, of course. In conventional Christian terms, she was a sinner, an adulteress who abandoned her husband and wandered from the true faith. Lord Coggan, the former Archbishop of Canterbury, branded her 'a false goddess with loose morals'.[2] Nevertheless, the astonishing public reaction to her death indicated that some kind of apotheosis had taken place. By common consent, London had never seen anything quite like it before. The funeral of the Princess of Wales, which was the culmination of a week of unprecedented national mourning, was watched by millions all round the world. For grief at the loss of Diana was not just a British, but a global phenomenon. This is evident from the fact that thirty countries issued Diana commemorative stamps within a month of her death.

For a year thereafter, barely a day passed without a story or a picture of Diana in the newspapers. Already iconic in her existence as an incomparable media celebrity, Diana's image now resonated for many with an almost unbearable beatitude. We have seen Italian Christmas cribs with a painted figurine of Diana lining up with the shepherds and Wise Men, and private shrines to Diana. We have heard Diana's brother ask that Diana should not be turned into a saint, only for him to construct an island shrine to her memory. And we have read the conservative Catholic Paul Johnson confess in *The Spectator* to praying to Diana.

Somehow, Diana had paid, with her life and her suffering, for the desires of others. One of the most striking sights in recent British history was that sea of flowers engulfing the approaches to Kensington Palace. It was as if the heavens had opened and flowers rained from the sky, seemingly without end. But each bouquet was a testament to someone's sorrow, someone's sense of personal grief and loss. This was part of a collective sense of loss for something the collective never possessed yet, paradoxically, claimed at the very moment of grief. In death, Diana became a figure of paradox: the People's Princess whose death became the catalyst for 'the floral revolution'.

It is in precisely such a contradictory way that Diana's 'saintly' dimension is announced. After she died, Diana's life, and her image, are seen to have stood for something that had been lacking: nationalism, communal spirit, generosity, love, emotionalism, even religious feeling and Christian values. Paul Johnson proclaimed that 'the effect of Diana's short life did more to promote Christian values in this country than all the efforts of our state Church in half a century. She made people, especially the poor, think seriously about what life is about. Despite her silly, pleasure-loving side, she was the grace of anti-materialism made flesh'.[3] Princess Diana, once the very embodiment of Madonna's Material Girl is seen, in death, in a very different, far less hedonistic guise. Even the Church of England acknowledged that Diana seemed to encapsulate or galvanise a sense of spiritual feeling, an implicit Christianity which the church must try to make explicit.[4]

Secular and more political accounts took the same, contradictory form. Among the plethora of Diana publications which appeared within a few weeks of her death, Beatrix Campbell and Julie Burchill produced books canonising Diana as a feminist heroine, the symbol of modern independent womanhood victimised by male patriarchy and a reactionary royal establishment. But other feminists were less enthusiastic: 'An over-privileged airhead', a 'Princess in Versace'. Joan Smith declared: 'There could hardly be a more vivid illustration of our deluded state, of our attachment to a kind of *faux*-modernity, than our readiness to canonise a woman whose dynastic ambitions, occasional good works - she left nothing to charity in her will - and sentimental aspirations would not be out of place in a Jane Austen novel'.[5] Similarly, commentators could not make up their mind whether the People's Princess embodied the spirit of Republicanism or a rejuvenated, modernised monarchy.

Diana's death on 31 August 1997 occurred at a significant moment in British history. The previous 1 May, New Labour had won a sweeping victory at the polls to end eighteen years of

Conservative rule. Labour was promising a new beginning and a new national identity. But this only added to the crisis of identity which had gripped Britain as the millennium approached. Home Rule for Scotland, Wales and Northern Ireland, the final demise of Empire with the handing back of Hong Kong to China on 30 June 1997, the uncertain role of Britain within Europe, all placed a question mark over the nature and future of the United Kingdom. Does the fact that, shortly before the 1997 election, a Gallup poll revealed that 48% of the population wished to emigrate suggest a deep sense of unease and unhappiness among the population at large? And did Diana, in death, provide a point of unity, reversing a sense of national fragmentation?

Diana, however, was not only 'England's rose'. Supremely, Diana's public role as the head of a number of charities and her work with children, the sick, AIDS patients, victims of land mines and so on, gave the impression that she was a global healer, at least in a metaphorical or symbolic sense, and lent to her image a halo of saintliness. Indeed, essentially, the variety of narratives that have taken shape since her death all take the form of hagiography. Whether she is seen as a feminist icon, a symbol of maternal love or single motherhood, a nationalist heroine, a sign of hope for the dispossessed and the suffering around the globe, a unifying point of identification for minority groups and the marginalised, the lonely, the poor, the sick, Diana is always turned into a saint – a postmodern saint. It is not only because her beatitude is contradictory and constructed in a multiplicity of differing narratives (which refuse the imposition of one grand narrative) that Diana's unofficial canonisation can be construed as postmodern. For Edith Wyschogrod, postmodern 'saintliness is not a nostalgic return to premodern hagiography but [an] expression of excessive desire, a desire on behalf of the Other that seeks the cessation of another's suffering and the birth of another's joy'.[6] Diana as a saintly figure of desire fits better than Diana as a saintly figure of asceticism, abnegation or self-negation. It is not simply that Diana expressed a wish to help others, but also that, in the multiple hagiographic accounts, Diana appears as a figure *of* desire – someone supposed to fill the lack in being that is manifested as suffering. Diana was both desired and desiring. And Diana bore the burden of an excessive desire of the Other, born out in the shocking explosion of grief at her death.

In her account of postmodern sainthood, Wyschogrod claims that the saint offers a model for ethical conduct, or at least a relation to an ethical existence, in a postmodern scene devoid of rationalist or theological foundation. To this extent, the saintly model is paradoxical because the saint's sanctity is not, indeed must not be, exclusively guaranteed by any particular institutionalised faith. Wyschogrod writes: 'Saints' lives should not be imagined as emanating from some specific religious community, but as found across a broad spectrum of belief systems and institutional practices. A saintly life is defined as one in which compassion for the Other, irrespective of cost to the saint, is the primary trait'.[7] Consequently, the lives of saints inevitably unfold in tension with the institutional frameworks that function as a background to their work, institutions that they may contest and confound, even if they are eventually re-absorbed by them. Sainthood is inseparable from the hagiographies that recognise them as such; insofar as the saint must function as an exemplar, his or her existence is bound up with representation and hagiographic forms of representation. In this sense, it makes no difference if the saint intended or wanted or desired to be a saint; insofar as he or she becomes the object of hagiographic desire, a saint is what she or he becomes. Indeed, the saint may be totally fictional.

But is this postmodern? Religious communities have often fabricated hagiographies for saints who never existed. Pierre Delooz, speaking of the Roman Catholic tradition, argues that, essentially, all saints, whether they actually existed or not, are constructed, they are 'manufactured', not born: 'Most saints were once real people, about whom objective facts may be established: their sex, their place of birth, and particularly of their death . . . But beside the real saints are what we call the *constructed* saints. All saints are more or less *constructed* in that, being necessarily saints for *other people*, they are remodelled in the collective representation which is made for them.'[8] It is not simply that, in order to be canonised, a saint must put himself or herself totally at the disposal of the Other, in the shape of the wretched of the Earth. It is rather that the saint is an object that is imagined to be totally at one's disposal, should one need it. The saint is an absolutely indispensable, disposable object, at once essential and yet dispensable. He or she is as fundamental, in a way, as the daily newspaper or TV news bulletin, that is here today and gone tomorrow, yet creating a sense of imagined community and providing the nation with some kind of unifying narrative. To this extent, Saint Diana is a product of the very media that exploited her.

Diana Spencer was continually put at the disposal of the Other, that is, she was made totally accessible and transparent to the Other in the shape of the consumers of media images around the globe. Her image is totally promiscuous; hers was the world's most saleable image before her death, and its value and ubiquity has vastly increased since. There is something almost pornographic about the glossy banality of Diana's endlessly reproduced image, and in the manipulation of public emotion that the media, in utilising these images, seeks in order to increase their sales figures. But this also contributes to the construction of Diana as a saint. Again, it is not simply because *kitsch* imagery has become the preferred mode of popular iconography, but because, as Wyschogrod suggests, hagiography overlaps with a 'discourse of depravity'.[9]

The image of Diana is bulimic in the sense that it typifies both excess and deprivation. Diana links images of deprivation, sickness, starvation and disability to conspicuous consumption. Ordinary folk in the West like to give to charity by consuming images of Diana, pop records, comedy shows, T-shirts and so on, while the rich folk like to fund-raise by throwing expensive parties in New York or Beverley Hills. In the West, charitable giving depends on the generation of desire: it turns sanctity into excessive consumption, makes it synonymous with the 'discourse of depravity'. Saint Diana, then, is also Our Lady of the Flowers, as much Saint Genet as Saint Teresa of Jesus. From this perspective, she is the masturbatory focus of a self-pleasuring altruism, an equivalent of the debauched guttersnipe of Jean-Paul Sartre's existentialist hagiography, where asceticism becomes total and unrestrained sexual indulgence.

The pornography of Diana's imaging in the media meets the point of absolute obscenity precisely at the moment when it becomes sanctified in death. The car crash in Paris was the ultimate in death-as-infotainment, in which death is hierarchised or rendered visible to the degree to which it is sensational and therefore 'newsworthy'. Speaking of 'the *death event*' as the 'new historical horizon', Wyschogrod suggests that disasters and newsworthy deaths constitute the often unconscious apperceptive background of daily existence. Life is held cheap. When natural calamity occurs, the affective responses to it are blunted, even when efforts to mitigate suffering are mobilised. Thus earthquake, the AIDS epidemic, famine, and other disasters strike without the resonance of awe that accompanied previous disasters.[10] Even though it was equivalent to these de-sensitised, mediatised disasters, the death of Diana transcends them. Diana's death transcended private tragedy in the same way that, to the media, it was more significant than those of Dodi Fayed and Henri Paul. Yet, at the same time, their proximity to Diana has led to *more* media significance being given to the life and death of Dodi Fayed, and more enigmatic notoriety to Henri Paul. In this way, Diana's death illuminates the plight of the sick, of AIDS sufferers, the victims of land mines, and so on, not just because she patronised their cause but because her death and suffering has become continuous with theirs: it provides anonymous suffering with the focus and definition of an empathetic personality, in the mediatised sense of the term. It is for this reason that, to be truly effective, a postmodern saint must also bear the burden of celebrity, whether she be Princess Diana or Mother Teresa.

*     *     *

This book is not a hagiography of Saint Diana, though Diana-hagiographies are its subject. It is a work that owes its origins to a small one-day colloquium held by Lancaster University in November 1997. Organised jointly by the Institute of Cultural Research and Women's Studies, it was among the first academic events to focus on the significance of the life and death of Diana. It was attended by some fifty interested scholars, who heard papers and debated the issues. For some, it was a genuine academic analysis of a phenomenon; for others, an opportunity to articulate and understand their own reactions to the events. It reflected the fact that scholars and academics were as much taken by surprise by the phenomenon of Diana's funeral as everyone else. In academic terms, its significance was similar to that of the Falklands War in 1982. At the time of the War, many academics could not understand the enormous popular support for what they saw as an anachronistic imperialist adventure. This led to a plethora of books, articles, conferences and essays on the subjects of patriotism, nationalism and national identity, subjects conspicuously absent from the scholarly agenda up to that point. That awakened interest has continued unabated to the present day.

Similarly, academics had for the first time in years become interested in the subject of the monarchy as the marriage of the Prince and Princess of Wales slowly and painfully unravelled. That interest quickened in the aftermath of the death and the funeral. It was reinforced by a desire to understand and explain the whole Diana phenomenon, her global appeal, her cultural significance, her political, religious and personal impact. Other conferences followed at the universities of Kent, Sussex and East London. The Free University of Berlin immediately put on a series of lectures on Diana.[11] Swansea University has now announced what appears to be the first regular taught course on Diana, a ten-week lecture course in the Adult Education Department on 'Diana: her life and impact'.[12] In addition there have been books about Diana, an estimated fifty in the first year following her death, ranging from photographic tributes to political polemics.[13]

The posthumous interest of the media reached a crescendo on the first anniversary of the death on 31 August 1998. Every television channel ran a documentary programme, several of them more than one, examining every aspect of her life and death. The newspapers published voluminous retrospectives of her life one year on. This caused one disgruntled paperboy to write to *The Independent* to say that he was sick of Princess Diana, and to complain about the weight of his paper bag.[14] His burden implicitly raises the question of the suffering of those having to bear the emotion of all the Diana mourners. Not everyone believed. Not everyone could understand or sympathise with the excessive mourning. This lack of love and grief did not emerge clearly at the time of the funeral, but it began to surface twelve months later. The political journalist Matthew Parris recalled that, returning with friends from South America after Diana's death, he felt a sense of being 'separated. One felt distanced, alienated. Our countrymen were seized by something with which we could not connect . . . We were far from alone . . . There was, and still is, a big, silent majority in Britain on the Princess . . . We did not know her, do not belittle her and can feel at her death only the respectful but reserved regret one feels at the death of any important stranger'.[15]

In a book on 'Saint Diana', it is important to allow dissenting voices to question Diana's iconicity, and to note the emergence of a range of dissenting views about the nature and extent of the Diana phenomenon. In a recent collection of essays entitled *Unbelievable*, for example, the editor Ian Jack questions the authenticity of the outpouring of grief over Diana's death, and speaks of 'recreational grieving'.[16] Diana's funeral was, he claims, 'grief-lite'. It was enjoyable, as being part of a large like-minded crowd is enjoyable. Likewise, documentaries like

ITV's 'The People's Princess', made up of footage shot during the lead up to, and staging of, the funeral itself and shown on the first anniversary, have tried to suggest that the motives of those attending were far from uniform or indeed reverent. Some of those interviewed admitted they had come for the spectacle and a day out. Others reported drunkenness and fighting in the crowd as it waited through the night, giving the whole event an unexpected element of the carnivalesque. It is claimed that 41% of the British population did not even watch the funeral on television. On the basis of a Gallup Poll taken as the first anniversary approached, *The Daily Telegraph* pronounced the onset of Diana fatigue; 93% of those polled planned no personal act of commemoration and only 28% favoured a national ceremony of remembrance.[17] An anniversary charity walk along the funeral route attracted only 300 people instead of the expected 15,000.

Another suggestion which emerges in *Unbelievable* is that the mourning for Diana was confined to particular social groups. It was, one contributor says, 'a C1, C2 and D phenomenon'. Others have suggested that a close look at the mourning crowds and analysis of *vox pop* interviews reveals the prominence of three groups in particular: women, gays and ethnic minorities. It was notable that the majority of those queuing to sign the books of condolence were women. Diana may have become a symbol and role model for young women under forty, as a single mother trying to carve out a new life and new relationships following a broken marriage. It was an experience many shared and one with which they empathised. Did groups who felt themselves marginalised by society identify with her in particular? There were the homeless whom she regularly visited, gays who loved her for trying to dispel the fear of AIDS, and members of ethnic minorities who were the victims of racism and discrimination. The sight of black men and women sobbing uncontrollably outside Buckingham Palace during the week after her death was particularly striking.

Other dissidents speak of the events surrounding Diana's death in terms of the effects of 'crowd psychology', 'mass sentiment', and even fascism - 'floral fascism', to use Maggie Winkworth's phrase. *The Guardian*'s Isabel Hilton felt that 'if a powerful demagogue had arisen from the crowd they would have stormed the palace gates'.[18]

The complaint seems to be the irrationality and suggestibility of the Diana phenomenon, and the naked and unreasoned emotionality of it all. The role of the media in generating mass emotion is beginning to be considered. And the argument that Diana unleashed a very unBritish affectivity, an style of emotional display more fitted to the other side of the Atlantic, is often rehearsed.

Then again, some dissidents explain the emotional outpouring as having more to do with guilt than grief. In the immediate aftermath of the crash, there seemed to be a desperate search for a scapegoat. Initially, it was the press and, in particular, the paparazzi who were said to have hounded Diana to her death. Earl Spencer's emotional denunciation of the press in his funeral oration turned him briefly into a popular hero, the 'People's Earl', until press reports of his divorce later revealed him as a serial adulterer who had driven his bulimic wife into a nursing home. In the aftermath of the crash, 85% of the population called for tighter privacy laws. Was it a classic case of transference of guilt? The people's own hunger for the often intrusive Diana stories had, after all, fuelled the press pursuit of Diana exclusives. The eagerness with which such stories were consumed dictated the continuing supply. The situation became more complicated when it was revealed that a drunken speeding driver - Henri Paul - was probably to blame for the crash. But Paul was already dead. So criticism was turned on the Queen and the royal family, who were at Balmoral on their regular summer break, and were denounced for not returning to London immediately to parade their grief in public. Hectoring tabloid headlines demanded of the Queen 'Show us your grief' and a ghoulish placard in the funeral crowd read 'William and Harry - please cry'. It can be argued that the vehemence of such criticism suggests a subconscious feeling of guilt at having sanctioned the pursuit of the Princess by the desire for the very stories which had apparently led to her untimely demise.

Whilst this volume ends with two chapters (by Simon Critchley and Alvin Cohan) which embody some of the questioning about the reality of Diana's iconicity, it is not our intention to develop or evaluate such dissident arguments at length. Already this important work is beginning to be undertaken elsewhere. To give just one example, in a recent issue of *Folklore*, Lucy Biddle and Tony Walter analyse what the Diana phenomenon reveals about 'emotional reserve and the English way of grief', and develop some important clarifications.[19] Against the argument that Diana's death points to the triumph of 'expressive grief' over 'private grief', they show that the latter was far from overwhelmed. The teddy bears and flowers left as tributes were emblems used to signify grief, not emotionality itself; few people broke down at the funeral, indeed an uncanny silence reigned; William and Harry were applauded for their courageous emotional control; Earl Spencer betrayed emotion only by a momentary crack in his voice. Despite the emotional 'invigilation' of the press, therefore, Biddle and Walter suggest that we witnessed not the triumph of expressive grief, but 'the ingredients of a perfected private grief'.

We look forward to more work of this kind. We have rehearsed the dissident arguments not in order to interrogate them, but in order to draw them to our readers' attention and set them alongside what follows. In the absence of further research, they must hang like unanswered questions and unconfirmed hypotheses over the massive and seemingly contradictory evidence of Diana's iconic status. Much of this evidence is discussed in the pieces which follow. It includes the proofs already surveyed in this introduction, and the facts which have now become familiar to us all: blanket news coverage of the death, 31.5 million viewers of Diana's funeral in Britain and an estimated 1 billion world-wide, the carpets of flowers, the sale of 40 million copies of 'Good-bye England's Rose', over £100 million donated to Diana's Memorial Fund, and polls which, even a year after her death, showed that many still believed themselves and their country to have been significantly changed by the Diana phenomenon; when asked about the idea of a 'post-Diana' society, for example, 41% said the country was now 'more caring and compassionate'[20]. A volume of 1500 poems by people of all ages testifying to their love and grief for the Princess has recently been published by Anchor Books, 'a people's poetry imprint'.

The muted nature of the first anniversary of the death may be explained in part by the fact that it occurred shortly after the Omagh bombing, which left 28 dead and 200 injured, and overtook the remembered grief for one person.

These facts are remarkable. The dissident facts that many people did not mourn and seemed not to have cared, that they saw Diana as nothing but an empty-headed bimbo or a sinful temptress, and that they declined to worship at the shrine of Saint Diana, must be included in any fair assessment of the Diana phenomenon, but do not subvert it. Diana was iconic because she symbolised, refracted, and focused so many of the values, hopes, and ideals which so many of us seem to cherish. Two years on from her death, we may be in a better position to begin to understand something of this iconicity.

\*   \*   \*

The theme of Diana as postmodern icon runs through many of the essays which follow. **Rosalind Brunt** opens the collection with an overview of the process by which Diana came to assume iconic status. She traces the trajectory of the notion of 'icon' itself, and notes how, particularly through its linkage with Diana, the word becomes part of everyday discourse by the time of her death. In keeping with the theme of late-, high- or post-modernity as 'reflexive' (see the work of Anthony Giddens and Ulrich Beck, for example), Brunt suggests that the entry of 'icon' into the vernacular tells us something about how new interpretations of the iconic are bound up with the democratisation of cultural studies. Brunt's chapter also serves to highlight the key role played by feminist writers in the development and analysis of Diana's iconic status, and discusses alternative assessments of Diana's iconic womanhood. On the one hand Diana was seen by some commentators as an icon of limited and restrictive images of womanhood – the child-woman, literally 'wedded' to her fate, restricted to 'choices within the family', broken and pitiable. On the other hand, she was regarded as subversive of such images – a symbol of women's strength and autonomy, courageous, subversive and triumphant, the new feminist icon celebrated by Burchill and Campbell. Finally, however, Brunt ends her chapter by noting that the point at which Diana's iconicity enters the vernacular is the point at which it embraces the numinous and re-acquires a religious meaning, a theme which is taken up by Paul Heelas and Linda Woodhead.

Continuing the theme of Diana as postmodern icon, **Scott Wilson** opens his chapter with a Sadean and Lacanian reflection on Diana as embodiment of beauty, excess, desire and death. Her beauty served to maintain and even provoke the spectacle of suffering for our delectation. Death crystallised the iconic image. Diana both inhabited a fictional space of imagined freedom in which celebrities disport themselves – and also a vale of tears, restrictions and tragedy. For Lacan, the saint carries the collectivity's questioning of existence and its death-driven desire in his or her own visible suffering. The collectivity 'consumes' this suffering, as Christ's body and blood is consumed at the eucharist. In the same way, we consumed Diana's suffering, and we grieved by consuming – by buying flowers, records, papers, magazines. Wilson's reflections thus lead on to a consideration of the situatedness of Diana's iconicity in the context of global capitalism. He considers both the 'consecration of consumption' in the cult of Diana, and the indispensable role of the media. Today, an event becomes historical because of the numbers who view or participate in it ; we make history through our knowing and willing participation in the sign. The media become the indispensable agents of iconicity: 'to the end, Diana's face was covered by the dazzling images that immortalised her'. Likewise, the celebrity and celebrity event have invaded the locus of the sacred: 'this radical shift', comments Wilson, 'was never better exemplified than by the wave of applause that issued from the crowds outside Westminster Abbey during Diana's funeral service, and swept through the august congregation turning it into a different kind of event entirely: a rock concert, perhaps, or, maybe, people thought, hoped even, a political rally'. Yet, he argues, this event was not truly political, and Diana did not usher in a new political dispensation or inaugurate a more caring society. Instead, the cult of Saint Diana merely reinforces the economy of consumption and a politics which makes recourse to emotions rather than information. 'Diana', he concludes, 'has become a powerfully maternal, superegoic figure who pins the politics of victimhood to the imperative to consume'.

The role of new media of communication and entertainment in the creation of Saint Diana is also considered by **Jeffrey Richards** in his chapter on 'The Hollywoodisation of Diana'. Richards argues that cinema had prepared the way for Diana's iconicity, both by constructing iconic points of reference in terms of which she could be understood, and by offering the ready-made roles of celebrity and 'everyday star' by which she could construct her own self-identity. Diana's stardom was reinforced by the creation of movies about her life, a genre whose development Richards documents in detail. Finally, Richards considers the long-standing relationship between Hollywood and royalty, and the tension in the depiction of the latter between mythologisation and humanisation. In Richard's view, the relationship between cinema and royalty has been mutually beneficial – and continued to be so even in the case of Diana. Richards believes that ultimately, Diana did nothing to weaken the British public's long-standing loyalty to the institution of monarchy, and that her royal status was the necessary foundation of her iconic status. 'Diana, mythologised in life and death, remains a star and her star status reinforces and strengthens the system of monarchy'.

**Emily Lomax** concentrates on the issue of Diana's iconic status in relation to national and ethnic identities. After reviewing different racialised reactions to Diana and Mohamed and Dodi Al-Fayed, Diana and Imran Khan, and Diana and her other 'foreign' partners, Lomax considers the interplay between two very different images of Diana: the transracial, transcultural icon of multiculturalism, and 'England's rose'. The Diana phenomenon, she suggests, can be viewed as 'a symptom of anxieties produced at the interstices of nation, race and culture in the global economy'. Instead of viewing the two Dianas as contradictory, Lomax points out how global capitalism encourages them and encourages an interplay between universalism and difference, for the arousal of desire for the exotic is the motor of consumption. As Lomax puts it, 'Capital's own transgressive progress depends upon constructing a 'transgressive Other' to fuel consumer desire, either as a point of exotic difference or as a point of prohibition, an imagined barrier, a veil, to that desire. These days ,difference, alterity, even the sacred itself is located in transgression'. Far from embracing the image of Diana as a multicultural icon, ushering in a new era of British politics and a new age of racial harmony, Lomax therefore remains suspicious. For her, Saint Diana becomes a crutch for a disintegrating sense of national identity and a cog in the global marketing machine. Diana is, moreover, a packaged commodity 'in which British identity is sold to the British people in precisely the way that Mohamed Al-Fayed attempted to buy it'. It is, Lomax argues, a measure of the racism that still exists in British society that the transaction is condemned in the case of Al-Fayed, an Egyptian, but not in relation to the British people. With reference to the debate about modernity and postmodernity, Lomax's chapter is interesting because it reveals the way in which Diana's iconicity interplays the two. The nation is, of course, the defining political frame of modernity. Today the nation is both threatened and redefined by the more 'postmodern' forces of globalisation. Diana's iconicity, as Lomax shows so well, relates equally to both.

For those for whom postmodernity is defined by eclectic consumerism and the collapse of overarching meta-narratives, norms and belief systems, **Paul Heelas'** chapter on 'Diana's Self and the Quest Within' continues the theme of the Princess as postmodern icon. In this case, however, it is not the way in which Diana was consumed by the forces of global capitalism that is of interest, but the way in which she herself became a 'spiritual shopper', drawing eclectically on a range of spiritual and self-help practices, beliefs, systems and techniques ranging from astrology to deep tissue massage to the New Age teachings of Deepak Chopra. Heelas suggests that Diana may be revealing of the way in which such instrumentalised, postmodern spiritual shopping is becoming the norm in contemporary society.

The main thrust of Heelas' chapter, however, leads not to an affirmation of Diana as a postmodern, but as *modern* icon. Heelas' central argument is that Diana's quest was the typically modern quest *within*, the quest to find one's true Self, to get in touch with the god within, to harness one's true potentiality, and 'realise the real me'. Diana, in other words, belonged to the 'expressive' strand of modern culture, the strand identified and analysed by theorists such as Edward Shils, Steven Tipton, Charles Taylor, and Robert Bellah.[21] Central to Western modernity, this cultural trajectory can be traced back to the Romantic movement of the late eighteenth and early nineteenth centuries. Not for Diana or her fellow questers the deconstruction or decentering of the self (that perennial theme of postmodern discourse). The only self that Diana and other New Agers wish to deconstruct is the 'social self', the self constructed by an iron cage of social expectations and empty and inauthentic traditions and rituals – a carapace which must be pierced in order to allow the true Self to emerge. Heelas argues that Diana's growing concern with New Age teaching and practices made it highly likely that she would have gone on to become an icon of the New Age movement, but her death 'brought to "life" all those of the population who would never dream of describing themselves as spiritual beings, but who nevertheless have faith in what their personal lives have to offer'; 'her way of "being" could thus resonate with all those who sense - albeit inchoately - that spirituality lies at the heart of what it is to be human'.

Continuing the theme of Diana as modern icon, **Linda Woodhead**'s chapter also considers Diana as symbol, symptom and icon of contemporary religiosity. But where Heelas found self-spirituality, Woodhead finds a more relational spirituality which she names the 'Religion of the Heart'. Departing from the more 'external' ritualistic, institutional and hierarchical elements of Christianity, the Religion of the Heart retains an emphasis on the importance of loving-kindness. It is, however, more deeply affective than traditional Christian 'charity', more optimistic in its view of human nature, and less interested in self-sacrifice. Drawing a contrast with Mother

Teresa's approach to religion, Woodhead argues that, 'Where Diana looked within to find God, Mother Teresa looked up; where Diana saw human loveliness, Mother Teresa saw sinful humanity; and where Diana saw uniquely valuable human beings, Mother Teresa saw Christ'. For Woodhead it is in its emphasis on the human and in its reliance on the discourses of humanitarianism that the modern (rationalistic Enlightenment) roots of Diana's brand of religiosity can be is found. Yet in its emphasis on the heart rather than reason, Diana's religion of humanity also draws on Romantic, expressive values. A mix of pre-modern Christian and modern Enlightenment and Romantic elements, Woodhead believes that this Religion of the Heart may have become the most influential form of faith in Western societies today. It is the religion practised by all those who value love above all other virtues, who find significance in intimate human relationships and humanitarian causes, and who believe that religion consists of kind deeds rather than clever words or correct doctrines. For all such, the icon of true religion – the heart – is now absorbed into a new super-icon: Diana, the Queen of Hearts. As a tribute left at Kensington Palace and quoted by Woodhead put it,

> *Saint DIANA*
>
> *THE IRREPLACEABLE PATRON SAINT OF LOVE*
>
> *In Our Hearts Forever.*

The essays in this collection thus reveal Diana as both modern and postmodern icon. More than that, however, they show that important elements of the pre-modern survive in this iconic figure. As Richards and Woodhead show, many scripts which appear modern or postmodern, recently invented and transparent in their meaning, are in fact more like palimpsests that contain overlays of much earlier writing. Just as tradition is ceaselessly modernised, so modernity and postmodernity are ceaselessly traditionalised. There is the continuing – if transformed – influence of Christianity on Diana. There is the undeniably important fact that Diana was a princess and was born a member of an ancient aristocracy. Likewise, as Richards argues, there is the importance of Diana's royal connection in triggering a number of medieval mythic images, not least that of the royal as anointed representative of God able to cure by the laying on of hands, as was once the case in monarchs 'touching for the King's evil', and of the saint whose shrine becomes the object of pilgrimage and whose relics become prized and powerful possessions.

Richard Fenn's chapter on 'Princess Diana as Lady Folly' continues these themes. 'It is tempting, but too facile', he argues, 'to suggest that Diana was the hallmark of Britain's entry into postmodernity, where fashions, friends, ideas, moods, and personalities engage in a constant game of mix and match ... to follow these suggestions is to be blind to the presence of the past ...'. Diana, he suggests, was acting out a role, one described in detail by Erasmus, that is actually a composite of many roles: court jester, fool, saint, masker, actor, carnivalgoer, ecstatic, and lover of souls. More than an unwitting exemplar of these social types, however, Diana also demonstrated the perennial function of play and humour, of compassion and disclosure, of whatever gives heart to a heartless world: 'In concert with certain Christian symbols and memories, beliefs and assumptions ... the roles of Lady Folly form a cultural template that has long been subversive in pointing to a more genial and humane sort of kingdom and in emphasising the alienating aspects of any social order'. As Lady Folly, Fenn sees Diana as an incalculable asset to the Royal Family, and their attempts to distance themselves from her as misguided: 'It is ... dangerous to part with Lady Folly, for the same reasons that it is dangerous for any social system to lose its capacity for self-criticism, its awareness of dissent and discontent, and its capacity to imagine another way of doing things'.

The volume ends with two short chapters which represent a shift in style and argument. Both were written soon after Diana's death, and both reflect on reactions to the death in autobiographical and anecdotal fashion. First, **Simon Critchley** recalls how, to his surprise, he found himself and others 'strangely moved' by Diana's death, and seeks explanations for this reaction. He finds an answer both in compassion (compassion felt for one who had herself known suffering and had felt compassion), and in a sense of the injustice, tragedy and meaninglessness of her death. The loss of this young woman who had been able to bring a sense of meaning to the lives of others raised the spectre of the meaningless in an unbearably painful way. People strove, vainly, to find some significance in the events. Diana, Critchley suggests, 'became some sort of universal lightening rod for people's sense of hurt, wrong and pain. People identified their pain with hers, and then reflected her obvious compassion with their own sense of compassion ...

and such compassion is not something apolitical, but rather an experience that might be said to contain within it the demand for political justice, for wrongs to be put right, for hurt to be heard, for personal pain to be assuaged by becoming public'.

Unlike Critchley, **Alvin Cohan** writes with the puzzled detachment of an outsider, someone struggling to understand the events surrounding Diana's death without being able to feel the emotion which others feel. Cohan's theme is the 'Spatial Diana', the physical places Diana 'occupied' in the weeks following her death. An American long-resident in Britain, Cohan begins by reflecting on how and where the news of Diana's death was communicated, and by comparing this with the dissemination of news about other momentous assassinations and deaths. This reflection leads Cohan to a comparison between reaction to Diana's death and reaction to the assassination of President Kennedy in 1963 and to the conclusion that whereas mourning for the latter was widespread and private, mourning for Diana was limited to certain designated spaces and was public. Cohan is a sceptic. He questions both the extent and the authenticity of the grief felt for Diana, and reminds us of the dissent over Diana's iconic status.

Through all its essays then, this book develops an argument. The argument is that Diana is a saint because she served to represent, focus, and enshrine values to which huge numbers of people made - and continue to make - obeisance. Her sainthood, however, is fragmented, disorganised, and contested. To the extent that she enshrines and focuses the values of charity, compassion, suffering, struggle, folly, and the power of the powerless, she may be called a Christian saint. To the extent that she enshrines and focuses the values of humanitarianism, romanticism, affectivity, consumption, and the cultivation of the self, she may be called a modern saint. Yet in and through all of this, she is undoubtedly a postmodern saint. She is postmodern as media saint, as saint of image, excess, beauty, desire and display. She is postmodern because she claims and is claimed by no one tradition or meta-narrative, and because she is a saint of the people and not the papacy. Above all, Diana is a postmodern saint because she enshrines, in riotous, contradictory, transforming, and disorganised fashion the conflicting values of the very different social and cultural dispensations which feed our times.[22]

# References

1   Cited in Edith Wyschogrod, *Saints and Postmodernism*, Chicago: University of Chicago Press, 1990, p. 31.
2   *Sunday Times*, 23rd August 1998, p. 1.
3   Paul Johnson, *The Spectator*, 29 August, 1998.
4   Bishop Michael Nazir-Ali in the *Church Times*, 24th November 1997, pp. 1 and 3.
5   Joan Smith, *Independent on Sunday*, 30 August, 1988.
6   Wyschogrod, *Saints and Postmodernism*, p. xxiv.
7   Wyschogrod, *Saints and Postmodernism*, p. xxiii.
8   Pierre Delooz, 'Toward a Sociological Study of Canonised Sainthood in the Catholic Church', in Stephen Wilson, ed., *Saints and their Cults: Studies in Religious Sociology, Folklore and History*, Cambridge: Cambridge University Press, 1983, p. 195.
9   Wyschogrod, *Saints and Postmodernism*, p. 191.
10  Wyschogrod, *Saints and Postmodernism*, p. xiv.
11  Wyschogrod, *Saints and Postmodernism*, p. xiv.
12  *South Wales Evening Post*, 12 September, 1998.
13  *Independent on Sunday*, 21 June, 1998.
14  *The Independent*, 31 August, 1998.
15  *The Times*, 31 August, 1998.
16  Ian Jack (ed.) *Granta 60: Unbelievable*, 1998. Quoted by Victoria Glendinning in her review of the book in *The Daily Telegraph*, 10 January, 1988, A3.
17  *Daily Telegraph*, 28 August, 1998.
18  Ian Jack (ed.) *Granta 60: Unbelievable*, 1998. Quoted by Victoria Glendinning in her review of the book in *The Daily Telegraph*, 10 January, 1988, A3.
19  *Folklore 109* (1998), pp. 96–99.
20  A special *Sunday Times*/NOP poll published 13 August, 1998 in *The Sunday Times*, p.1.
21  See Edward Shils, *Tradition*, London, Faber and Faber, 1981; Steven Tipton, *Getting Saved from the Sixties*, London, University of California Press, 1982; Charles Taylor, *The Ethics of Authenticity*, London, Harvard University Press, 1991; Robert Bellah, R. Madson, W. Sullivan, A. Swidler, and S. Tipton, *Habits of the Heart*, London, University of California Press, 1985.
22  There are, of course, many other aspects of Diana's iconicity which we would like to have covered in this volume, and which we hope will become the object of other studies. We would have liked to reflect further, for example, on Diana as a sexual icon. Her effect as a feminist role model or anti-hero is considered by Brunt. It would also have been interesting to consider, for example, her role as a gay icon. At the most obvious level, this derived from her public commitment to the plight of AIDS sufferers, and from her glamour. Equally, Diana, like other gay icons, achieved her status because she provided a public image of

suffering in and for personal relationships, at the hands of an 'Establishment'. Thus, Oscar Wilde, Judy Garland, Edith Piaf and Marilyn Monroe all feature in the gay pantheon, because they lived their emotional lives in the full glare of publicity, experienced the pain of rejection and died prematurely.

# 1. Princess Diana: A Sign of the Times

**Rosalind Brunt**

Five weeks before Princess Diana was killed, *The Observer* newspaper ran as its leading feature an article entitled, 'A trash icon for our times'. The article was based on a detailed interpretation of another newspaper's front page. In the middle of the previous week, *The Mirror*, using the headline 'Healing Hands', had splashed a colour blow-up photograph of Diana comforting the singer Elton John at the memorial service for the murdered fashion designer, Gianni Versace. To Nigel Fountain, the writer of *The Observer* piece, the Healing Hands image of Diana crystallised everything that was empty and ersatz about celebrity values and so, by extension, acted as 'a mirror for England' indicating 'the way we live now'.

> '*The Mirror's page wraps up times of global villaging and cultural plunder. Who needs Dada, surrealism, situationism, the society of the spectacle? We have, hot on the front page and fully post-modernist, our Tragedy Lite. Consider that image, quite unforeseeable and unbelievable two decades ago, as a statement of where we are now. The Queen of England manquée is sitting in a fourteenth century Piedmont cathedral, consoling a weeping, defunct, re-haired Seventies glam rocker about the murder of an Italian porno-frock-designing bondage freak by a Filipino-Californian gay hustler serial killer and/or Mafia hitperson who has since allegedly blown most of his own face off.*'[1]

Fountain goes on to contrast this image with famous photographs capturing wartime heroism and death. He writes allusively and rhetorically, creating momentum through an accumulation of speculative impressions which build up to the judgment that Princess Diana and Elton John together symbolise both the trivial ephemerality and 'schlock' aspects of the Nineties lifestyle. Calling them the duo 'Di and Dwight' (Reg Dwight being John's original name), Fountain describes the pair as mesmerising and stultifying 'us' - the English/British - in ways which divert us from engagement with the real and durable concerns of living:

> 'So there in the middle of it all, are Di and Dwight, a much loved quality British double act for the Nineties, icons for display in that global gallery of people whose native land is the airport; time does not pass but, locked in Groundhog Day, is endlessly recycled, like fugged air in a submarine'.

Fountain's repeated references to Hollywood serve to reinforce the hollowness of the scenario. But he also sees a more sinister aspect: behind Diana's popularity also lies the Hollywood-horror view of madness:

> 'After a while I figured out where I had seen Di's comforting expression before. It was Kathy Bates, the crazed fan/kidnapper of pulp writer James Caan in Stephen King's Misery, round about the time she realises he isn't happy with her favoured plot outline and gets serious about cracking his legs'.

At the end of July 1997, therefore, Diana can thus appear as the flash-trash, mad-bad emblem of a superficial, amoral and emptily post-modern Nineties. Only a month or so later, at the beginning of September 1997, in the immediate aftermath of her own death, Diana is being predominantly described as symbolising a quite contrary epochal image: the 'caring' feminised Nineties. The key epithets memorialising her qualities now highlight, not the *ersatz*, but the 'real' and the 'genuine' and far from being regarded in a demonic light as sinister and crazed, Diana is being evaluated according to various attributes of sanctity.

But what both these quite contrasting characterisations have in common is that they invoke Diana as an icon. She is perceived as iconic, first as some kind of celebrity, then according to some perceived aspect of her femininity along with some revelation about signs of the times. What I want to consider in this chapter are the diverse ways that iconic status came to accrue to Diana during her lifetime, as Princess of Wales. I'll therefore fill in some of the detail of a mythologising spectrum that can range from representing the 'demon of trash' to the 'saint of genuine feeling', and discuss how these characterisations are given epochal inflexions as messages for our age.

In looking at how Diana is perceived to embody these multiple and often contradictory themes, I also want to trace the trajectory of the notion of 'icon' itself and to note how, particularly through the linkage of the term with Diana, 'icon' becomes part of everyday discourse by the time of her death. Finally, if the making of Diana as icon is associated with the entry of 'icon' into the vernacular, I want to suggest that this says something about how the democratisation of cultural studies works to produce new interpretations of the iconic.

Diana's death and its immediate aftermath produced what Foucault, critiquing the notion of a repressed sexuality, characterised as 'an immense verbosity'.[2] In Diana's case too, the very excess of commentary and tribute indicates in itself a sort of challenge to Western taboos around death and dying, and a declaration that neither death nor sexuality is are ineffable. It was one of those occasions when 'everybody' could feel entitled to express a view and in this democracy of opinion-formation, nobody, whether members of the public or media commentators, confessed to be lost for words. The event produced an excess of analogy, expressing by simile or metaphor what the Princess was like, what her life and death signified to individuals, and what she had represented both nationally and globally. The key question asked of British people in *vox pops* broadcast during the week between the death and the funeral was: 'What did Princess Diana mean to you?' It invited a response that expressed both immediate subjective identity with the Princess and also wider social and cultural definition. Neither lay people nor public figures found the question odd or difficult to answer in personal or in social terms. If, as was usually the case, they had never met Princess Diana, they stressed that they felt *as if* they had known her and then went on to offer an interpretation of her iconic status. It seemed that everyone now felt quite competent and at home with forms of cultural and textual reading that had formerly been the province of academic and professional commentators.

The public discourse on Diana's significance could, however, also draw on an existing repertoire of imagery put into circulation during Diana's lifetime. This had been developed by a number of cultural critics who, like Fountain in *The Observer*, discussed the representation of Diana around the organising notion of 'icon'. Not surprisingly, it has been mainly feminist commentators familiar with media culture and cultural studies debates who have particularly worked on Diana's many iconic meanings as a way of responding to her status both as a royal and as a celebrity. It was they who drew attention to the point that, in joining the Royal Family, Diana had not merely 'become' royal, she was also clearly 'working' at it. There were elements of experiment and perform-ance in her public appearances and media representation that linked her assumption of royalty with the celebrity of stars; this made it appropriate to discuss Diana in iconic terms and increasingly, as having a "royal" with a persona fascinatingly distinct from the rest of the Family.

An early examination of Diana's appeal in these terms, and indeed the only book-length account to appear before her death, is Diana Simmonds, *Princess Di: The National Dish*, subtitled: 'The Making of a Media Star'.[3] The book draws on Simmonds' own journalistic background as a popular culture and television writer for the London listings magazine, *City Limits*. It deals with the period from September 1980 when the media first 'discovered' and then started tracking Lady Diana Spencer, to her engagement in February 1981 and wedding the following July . It suggests Diana reached 'global status' following a triumphant Australian tour with Prince Charles and the baby Prince William in 1983. It was this occasion which Simmonds marks as the moment when Diana's celebrity status first eclipsed Charles' royal role as future king.[4]

The book's cover design has a glamorous picture of Diana as if on a Heinz baked bean tin, but Simmonds does not make much of the consumerist and commodification implications of her own 'dish' conceit. The only time she uses her title phrase is when she points to a more general thesis about Diana's function as a political and cultural diversion:

> *'Little surprise....that the dream Princess, the fairy cake,*
> *the truly scrumptious national dish, should be fallen upon*
> *with such rapacious desperation by the press who informed*

*their readers day in and day out that the collective psyche*
*and imagination was starving for just such a distraction.*[5]

Simmonds' view of Diana as National Dish is that she provides a
form of 'mass psychic renewal' which serves as both a distraction
from the emiseration and heightened unemployment of the early
Thatcher years, as a consolation for the continued decline of Britain's
world status and a post-Falklands refusal 'to recognise what it has
become – a small aircraft carrier for the USA'.[6]

Within this wider political context, Simmonds concentrates on
what Diana exemplifies in terms of both traditional and modern
femininity:

> *'Diana Spencer, aristocrat, ordinary girl and scholastic*
> *failure has achieved the impossible status – not only of Fairy*
> *Princess and Virgin Mother, but also the magical Size Ten.*
> *She* is *the disastrous heroine of the eighties'.*[7]

What Simmonds means by 'disastrous' she discusses in terms of
women's magazine imagery. The Diana persona had managed to
by-pass two Seventies models of femininity: both of them were
exemplified by *Spare Rib*, the feminist magazine in an ironic 'Don't
Do It, Di' campaign before the Royal Wedding, and in the
Cosmopolitan version of glamorous career women heroines. Instead,
Simmonds had reverted to the more limiting ambition of wife and
mother whilst also literally incorporating the Ideal Body fantasy
prescribed by *Vogue* magazine. Simmonds notes how important
*Vogue*'s clothes and cosmetics advice were to the original creation of
Diana as 'media star'.[8] Her dismay is that Diana's early achievement
of the Vogue look sealed the Eighties 'having it all' goal offered to
Western women. Diana thus comes to stand as a reproach to the vast
majority of women who cannot live up to 'the impossible image which
every woman is taught to believe is perfection' and which 'imposes a
psychic burden which requires a monstrous effort to shift'.[9]

Rumours of Diana's own 'psychic burden' in achieving the
glamour and celebrity look were only unconfirmed press reports at
this stage. Later confirmation of eating disorders and low self-
esteem[10] would create a whole set of new identifications with women
in the Nineties. But even in this early period, Simmonds notes how
Diana could also overcome the reproach that her Ideal Body

represented the very 'ordinariness' of her appeal to women. Being perceived as 'ordinary' was, Simmonds suggests, a perverse way of being seen as 'extraordinary': Diana's ability to 'act naturally' and behave so reassuringly 'like us', whilst remaining so excessively glamorous and royal in the intense spotlight of public occasions, only served to enhance her stardom and celebrity.

Rosalind Coward's essay, 'The Royals'[11], published in the same year as Simmonds' book, covers the same early marriage period and examines similar themes of stardom and femininity. Coward, coming from an academic background that included a period at the Birmingham Centre for Contemporary Cultural Studies, was the first commentator to explore in detail the soap opera analogy that was to become a common comparison by the mid-Eighties. Coward describes how the media construction of 'The Royals' works as a family melodrama in ways similar to *Dallas*, the popular American soap opera of the time. Thus 'The Royals' and *Dallas* share a preoc-cupation with dynastic inheritance, narrative tension between the requirements of love and family duty, an excessive emphasis on sexual relations and marriage and a shifting cast of deserving and undeserving characters. But, she argues, a difference arises around their representations of feminine possibilities. Whereas the narra-tives of *Dallas* include some discourses of female independence that acknowledge, albeit in a contested way, other options for women besides marriage and motherhood, the story of 'The Royals', while presenting their key character, Diana, as a modern woman, simultaneously reduces all issues faced by modern women to 'choices within the family':

> *'... there's not a moment's hesitation in producing Lady Di as a modern heroine even though she married at twenty, was a mother by twenty-one, and had never had any sexual experience outside marriage.*

> *Not only does 'The Royals' accomplish a repression of ques-tions of female independence, it also accomplishes a repression of political and economic factors ...The way in which the story is told means that we never have to deal with the Royal Family as a political institution; we only have to think about human behaviours, human emotions, and choices restricted to the family. 'The Royals' eternalises traditional values, glorifies women's route to power through individual*

*sexual attraction, and defines women as exclusively bound up
with these values.'[12]*

Simmonds' suggestions of what happens with Diana as media star,
as echoed by Coward with her exploration of the royal soap opera,
imply that some form of cultural diversion from material issues and
the lives of real women is going on here. Beneath the veneer of Diana's
modern style, a traditionalist version of femininity is being
legitimated. However, the values it draws on are not static. Coward
emphasises how the same royal individuals may have projected onto
them a variety of positive/negative characteristics. In Diana's case,
she points out, the newly-married woman who started off as a Fairy
Princess soon comes to acquire the attributes of wilful wife getting
above her station and becoming the traditional nagging scold of the
dutiful, long-suffering husband.

The 'problem' of what can be culturally envisaged for Diana
after The Wedding is a theme addressed by the feminist novelist and
critic, Joan Smith, who reflects on the 1985-87 period, when
persistent rumours of marriage difficulties first surfaced. Smith
adopts another fictional analogy for Diana in her essay, 'The Frog
Princess' from her *Misogynies*[13] collection which acknowledges its
debt to Roland Barthes' cultural analyses of contemporary myth. In
the essay, Smith compares Diana, the romantic heroine of the 1981
engagement-wedding period with the eponymous heroine of
Georgette Heyer's Regency novel, *Arabella* (1964). She suggests that
the appeal of Diana-Arabella for Regency bucks, as much as for
Prince Charles and a present-day misogynistic culture, is that key
figure of arrested development: the child-woman. The 'problem' is
then what happens next. For romantic fantasy conventionally ends
with the wedding; its happy-ever-after assumptions typically
preserve the heroine as an innocent, inexperienced woman dependent
on the older and wiser hero. Imprisoned in 'the tinsel fantasy' of the
Royal Wedding, Smith argues, it is impossible for Diana to acquire
the symbols of grown-up womanhood without being represented as
wilful, unreasonable, spoiled and arrogant:

> '...it was always apparent, even during their courtship, that
> Charles and Diana were being created in the image of
> characters in fiction, that they were participants in a fragile
> fantasy which bore the warning of its own sell-by date. The

*union of youth and age, innocence and experience is an*
*unequal and therefore an unstable one; it is a teacher-pupil*
*relationship in which one partner is bound to change and the*
*other is not. Diana could not go on being Arabella ... But ...*
*the spectacle of Fleet Street making moral and financial*
*capital out of the demise of the dream they foisted upon her*
*is an unedifying one. There is a general lesson to be learned*
*here, a moral about the folly of trying to act out a tinsel*
*fantasy which denies adult status to women, but it is also a*
*cautionary tale about journalists (and) about a princess*
*who was kissed by Fleet Street and turned into a frog.*[14]

Joan Smith's own version of the sequel, the later essay, 'To Di for: The Queen of Broken Hearts', was published with unfortunate timing in her new collection, *Different for Girls: How Culture Creates Women*[15] during the week of Diana's death. It charts a Nineties Diana who has, after all, broken free of the media 'fairytale' and as a separated and then divorced woman takes charge of her own image. But Smith argues that Diana's self-promotion actually involved collusion with the media and consequently produced yet more misogynistic versions of traditional femininity. She examines in detail the 1992 Andrew Morton biography, *Diana, her True Life*, which, it was believed, had been written in some kind of close association with Diana,[16] and notes its repeated highlighting of a tearful, depressive victim status for the Princess: 'It is reasonable to assume not just that its lachrymose portrait of Diana is accurate but that, more to the point, this is how she wanted to be seen: as a fragile, pitiable figure, rather than a poised young woman'. Referring to Morton's sequel, *Diana: Her New Life*, published in 1995, two years after the separation from Charles, Smith takes issue with its title, suggesting that the book offers, rather, the impression of someone 'locked' into repeating an old life and showing no signs of moving on to a new , more independent female identity. Smith sees this impression reinforced in the *Panorama* interview Diana gave in November of the same year:[17]

*'The story she poured out could scarcely have been more*
*dramatic, involving deception, betrayal and despair in the*
*very highest circles, but there was no need simply to take her*
*word for it; what she was asking, in effect, was that people*

*should trust the evidence of their own eyes. Those very
viewers who remembered her as a glowing girl, descending
like Cinderella from her glass coach on the day of her
wedding in 1981, could see for themselves that she had been
transformed by her marriage into this haggard, slightly
dishevelled, rigidly controlled young woman ... This was
someone ... to whom terrible things had been done and whose
statement "I am strong" was contradicted at every turn by
language and visual cues which insisted "I am a victim" ...
she had exploited the directness and immediacy of television
to outflank her enemies and re-create herself as the
archetypal wronged woman. She was* la traviata *personified,
a latter-day* dame aux caméllias, *Anna Karenina after
Vronsky abandoned her."[18]*

Smith's account of Diana's post-marriage image is that she represents
a woman literally 'wedded' to her unhappy past. There can be no
'break' beyond the wedding, marriage, or any subsequent sexual alliance: all these events are doomed to be relived in the traditionalist
terms of a cycle of betrayal – whether by Charles, his lover, Camilla,
or Diana's lover, James Hewitt. From this perspective, Smith
provides extracts from Dickens' *Great Expectations* giving the hero's
account of meeting the long-abandoned bride, Miss Havisham, to
counterpoint Diana's 'wronged woman' narrative. Whilst
acknowledging the current popularity of Diana's 'Tragic Victim'
figure, she foresees the Diana image dwindling in the longer run to
all the pathos and ridicule that Miss Havisham evokes.

Smith's interpretation of Diana involves a conscious polemic
against more prevalent feminist versions of the Morton biographies
and the revelations of *Panorama*. But although she herself chooses to
highlight the conventionally romantic and tragic aspects of Diana's
femininity, she does acknowledge that there are other cultural readings available and put into media play by Diana herself:

*'The* Panorama *interview was much more than a blatantly
partisan account of her marriage; it marked her invention,
at a stroke, of a new and multifaceted identity for herself.
Appropriating the language of such disparate discourses as
traditional romance, psychotherapy and even feminism, she
had succeeded in reaching out to the broadest of all possible*

*constituencies – so much so that the then* Guardian
*columnist Suzanne Moore rushed into print hailing the
Princess, however improbably, as a heroine for the women's
movement.*[19]

Despite her recognition of Diana's 'multifaceted identity', Smith
cannot countenance its stretching so far as to become some kind of
feminist icon, and she goes on to dismiss Moore for the 'near-
canonisation' she performs on Diana, celebrating it with quotations
from the gay/feminist anthem, 'I Will Survive'.

But after Diana died, it was indeed the Suzanne Moore version
that predominated, with the late princess perceived as an exemplar
of women's strength and autonomy . In the week of mourning that
followed, Diana was claimed for mass female identification in
Moore's own columns in *The Independent*. The first two book-length
cultural analyses from feminist writers to be published in 1998 both
endorsed Moore's perspective on Diana. Beatrix Campbell, with
*Diana Princess of Wales*, subtitled, *How Sexual Politics Shook the
Monarchy*, and Julie Burchill, with *Diana*, both championed their
subject as a quasi-feminist survivor who called to account both
betraying men and a hostile, deeply patriarchal Royal Family.[20] This
theme was also echoed throughout the public mourning period, when
written tributes to the Princess simultaneously evinced anger with
the Royal Family, and took the line that Diana was best of the lot or
worth more than all the other royals put together.

The strong public partisanship demonstrated for Diana in this
period as a woman in her own right, divorced both from a bad marriage and her cold royal in-laws, was also aligned with themes of
popular and democratic culture evoked by the Prime Minister's
tribute, 'She *was* the people's Princess,' on the day of Diana's death.
The notion of 'The People's Princess' which was to inform so much
of the public mourning was first suggested to Tony Blair by his press
secretary, Alistair Campbell, who, as a former tabloid journalist was
well-attuned to definitions of public mood. But it was Julie Burchill,
a partisan for Diana long before she wrote her book, who first identified how Diana 'worked' in terms of popular culture.

In her 1992 essay, 'Di Hard: The Pop Princess', written in the
wake of the first Morton biography, *Diana, Her True Life*, Burchill
first defines Diana as a powerful celebrity figure comparable with two
other powerful, in-control 'stars', Margaret Thatcher and Madonna.[21]

But she then asserts that Diana now goes 'beyond' them and indeed all the Royal Family, because, emphatically, *'she is the point'*. Diana's 'point' is her iconic ability to inhabit popular culture and through it, relate to 'the people'. For Burchill, Diana is 'the first royal icon raised on and sustained by pop culture. She is our Pop Princess'.[22] Diana signals her 'popness' by her knowledge and open enjoyment of soap opera, romantic novels and advertising jingles: she challenges royal pomp with pop, apparently crooning 'Just One Cornetto' as she steps into the wedding coach. But she also demonstrates her pop credentials with a new emotional openness and spontaneity: 'Not for Diana the stiff upper lip and stiff G & T attitude to disappointments of the heart; she is as touchy-feely psychologically as she is physically'.[23]

Noting that 1991 was the first year that Diana took over from the Queen as the Royal Family's most popular member, Burchill praises her ability to perform. Being a great performer does not however render Diana inauthentic for performance is at the heart of celebrity and 'like all great stars she is only truly alive when performing'.[24] For Burchill, it is the very 'performance' of pop attributes that makes Diana both lovable and loved by the public. They also believe her to be 'of' the people and also happiest 'among' them. Anticipating the Blair tribute, Burchill concludes:

> ' *"Get a life"* goes the saying – and no one ever got a life as dramatically and drastically as she. Whether it is a life she will tolerate for ever we cannot know. But one thing is sure: whatever she does, for the first time ever the love and loyalty of the people has shifted irretrievably from the ruling house – until death, beyond divorce and dishonour – to one individual. To the one and only People's – and Pop's – Princess.'[25]

Burchill and all the other women commentators I have quoted discuss Diana in iconic terms firstly because they see her as the only member of the British Royal Family to achieve the celebrity of a modern media star; then, because she signifies something, whether positive or negative, about the changing status of women; and finally because her femininity and celebrity can be linked in some way to the state of the culture and signs of the times. Thus for instance, Diana Simmonds polemicises against a stultifying version of film studies for dissecting the star as icon in an abstract, textual way which divorces the notion from any social or political context. Her study of Diana as icon intends to restore historical specificity to the concept, and in a jokey preface that also mocks the jargon of cultural studies, she announces the aim of the book thus:

> *'So, in order to 'contextualise the princess within the existing cultural interface' - and to figure out where she fits in the scheme of things - this modest volume is offered both to enlighten and entertain ... Try not to skip to the naughty or fun bits. The history of the tribe is essential to any understanding of them and the collective British psyche.'* [26]

From this perspective, Simmonds interprets Diana's marriage to Charles, who thereby acquires a caring New Man guise following his repressed bachelor Action Man role, as an antidote to both the psychic and economic ravages of early Thatcherism. Simmonds also sees the Royal Wedding as reprising the glamorous fascination that Princess Elizabeth's marriage to Philip in 1947 created for Austerity Britain. And therein lies the danger she fears: for functioning as a fascination and an antidote may create the sort of glib diversion that prevents any direct confrontation with actual material circumstances.

Joan Smith's starting point for her interpretation of 'the history of the tribe' is the cultural climate surrounding the Yorkshire Ripper's serial murders of women in the late seventies. For Smith, the publicity and events surrounding the Ripper murders act like a touchstone revelation about the extent and depth of misogyny in contemporary Britain and western culture. The case studies of her essay collections feature women who, if not literally or metaphorically killed off, have been actually or figuratively reduced and undermined. In the introduction to her second book, Smith asks why, when women have made huge advances in both the public and private spheres, 'something still holds us back'. That 'something' she suggests, involves 'the messages we get from our culture about female behaviour', messages which invite women to fear that the taking of any real power will incur a devastating loss of femininity. These cultural messages include narratives about women who are at one extreme of the spectrum, the icons of femininity and at the other, the ogres, like the female murderers who remain unredeemable for transgressing against the ultimate taboo. Our current female icons, Smith suggests, betray a *fin de siècle* anxiety about women's aims for autonomy. She notes an obsessional fascination clustering around three major 'sad' and waiflike icons: Princess Diana, Marilyn Monroe and Jackie Kennedy and connects them thus:

> *'Each of them, in her own way, represents a type of femininity which is both out-of-date and extremely seductive - for women as well as for men - at a moment when the old certainties about gender no longer seem to apply. All three are soft, vulnerable and sad, so that we can admire them without feeling the envy that tougher sassier women like Madonna inspire. They are also, in a world in which our attitudes to powerful women like Hillary Clinton and Cherie Blair are equivocal to say the least, the standard against which we are all measured - and measure ourselves - to some degree ... Icons and ogres: these are the exemplars each culture uses to convey the boundaries that should not be crossed'.*[27]

Smith's remarks recall Simmonds' earlier view of the 'psychic burden' that the Diana icon imposes on women. Her emphasis is on a culture that uses both patriarchal and misogynistic means to define and patrol the boundaries of femininity and thus define for women who the icons and ogres are meant to be.

The last feminist commentator I want to consider is Camille Paglia, who identifies some of the same iconic strands of sadness and betrayal that Smith finds in the Diana image. Paglia, a professor of humanities based in Philadelphia, examines the iconic status of Diana in terms of the notion of cultural and sexual masks or *'personae'*. Her academic research has concentrated on how traces of *personae* from Roman, Greek and Egyptian myth have continued to reverberate within modern secular universes. Translating this research into journalistic commentary on present-day celebrities, she has argued for what she calls a 'revamped' feminism to celebrate not just the nice and the good women, but also include the bad girls the vampish and vampiric personae. Her studies of Diana include the essay, 'Diana Regina', reprinted in her collection, *Vamps and Tramps*. It was first published in 1992 as a response to the Morton's *Diana, her True Life* and formed the basis of the controversial British television programme, *Diana Unclothed*.[28]

Paglia's essay begins by acknowledging how the biography hugely inflamed interest in Diana:

*'It is an international obsession whose scale and longevity
show that it is more than high-class soap opera or a
reactionary wish-fulfillment fantasy..........those who have
never taken Diana seriously should take a new look. With
this latest burst of press attention, Diana may have become
the most powerful image in world popular culture
today..........It is increasingly obvious that Diana's story
taps into certain deep and powerful strains in our culture,
strains that suggest that the ancient archetypes of
conventional womanhood are not obsolete but stronger and
deeper than ever'.* [29]

Although highlighting here the 'conventional' images of femininity,
Paglia proceeds to transcend traditional/modern, victim/survivor
oppositions to present a thoroughly overdetermined and contradic-
tory icon of Diana which reprises and incorporates a range of clas-
sical and contemporary analogies. Included in Paglia's list are:
Cinderella, the betrayed wife, the ingenue Isobel Archer from Henry
James's *The Portrait of a Lady*, the princess in the tower, a pre-
Raphaelite heroine, the *mater dolorosa* - and here Paglia concurs with
Smith in aligning the Diana persona with that of Jackie Kennedy:
'With the powerful revelations of [Morton's] book Diana assumes
the international position once held by Jacqueline Kennedy ...
Suffering redeems and the world honours grace under pressure'.[30]
But the iconic image also contains the more vivid and forceful ele-
ments of the Hollywood queen, the last of the silent movie stars -
because Diana is more expressive as a visual and gestural presence
than as a public speaker - and the beautiful boy - because of her
provocatively androgynous appeal. But Paglia then wraps up all these
images into the dominant persona of the pagan goddess, Diana-
Artemis and concludes thus:

*'Diana's multiple* personae *from princess and mother to
Greek ephebe, are rich and far-ranging but also mutually
contradictory, and they are clearly consuming her. No one,
least of all a nervous, vulnerable young woman, could
sustain the voyeuristic laser beam of the world's adulation ...
The modern mega-celebrity, bearing the burden of collective
symbolism, projection, and fantasy, is a ritual victim, can-
nibalised by our pity and fear ... Mass media have made*

*both myth and disaster out of Diana's story. We have
created her in our own image. And pursued by our best
wishes, Diana the huntress is now the hind paralysed in the
world's gun-sight.'* [31]

A death foretold, albeit in symbolic terms. Like most of the women
writers I have discussed, Paglia's comments proved highly prescient
about themes that reappeared after Diana's death. Her conclusion is
echoed in Earl Spencer's references to the power of the media and to
the 'irony' of the Artemis story in his funeral tribute to Diana.[32] In
the immediate aftermath of Diana's death, many of the earlier iconic
strands re-emerged in the massed public messages that appeared at
focal points outside the royal palaces and nationwide. Notably, there
was a return to the earliest image, that of the 'fairytale princess'. But
this time, Charles had been replaced by the last lover, Dodi Fayed,
in a popularly imagined everlastingly happy unity of 'Di and Dodi'.

At the same time, the term 'icon' itself was being
unselfconsciously adopted into the vocabulary of everyday speech
and massively reinforced in the written tributes to Diana. To arrive
in the vernacular at the end of the twentieth century, the trajectory
of 'icon' had stretched through the academic fields of art history,
linguistics and semiology and thence into film studies and cultural
studies. Along the way, as part of C. S. Peirce's tripartite division of
the sign into icon, index and symbol, with 'icon' being, like a portrait,
the sign that most resembles its object, the term had become
particularly identified with the visual culture of photograph and film
and hence, used almost interchangeably with 'star'.[33] But in the
process, it had also taken on Peirce's notion of 'symbol' - the sign
associated with culture and convention. By the time Diana is being
represented in iconic terms, all these thematic resonances are in play.

In her 1985 essay, 'Royalty and Representation', Judith
Williamson develops the theme of the Royal Family as similar-but-
different from 'us'.[34] She adopts Peirce's notion of the 'index' as the
sign which has an existential association with its object, and, like
smoke is to fire, is an effect of what it stands for. Then taking his
distinction between 'icon' and 'index', she contrasts the iconic and
feudal nature of the British Royal Family with the indexical and
democratic nature of the American Presidency. She goes on to
compare monarchical and presidential representations thus:

> *'... despite their position at the very top of the social*
> *pyramid, or rather, because of it, the royal family* stand
> for, *or represent the broadest part of it, the popular, the*
> *masses of people who are not 'special' in any way. The*
> *American notion that anyone can become President means*
> *that their head of State not only stands for but also* shows
> *what the 'average person' can achieve. The President*
> *therefore functions as an* indexical *sign, a measure of*
> *something. However, the Royal Family is neither elected*
> *nor replaceable, nor could 'we' ever be 'them': they*
> *represent us by sheer* analogy, *an* iconic *sign, to pursue*
> *Peirce's categories. This way in which the Royal Family*
> parallels *our own , but at a distance, is the heart of its*
> *representative function'.*[35]

When it comes to representing the iconic quality of Diana, 'sheer analogy', as I've indicated, is also a matter of the increasing range and variety of analogy right up to Camille Paglia's image of an icon so over-freighted with meaning that it threatens to devour its subject. But in the aftermath of Diana's death, when the weight of analogy that has been developed in cultural commentary and journalism is poured into popular idiom, the notion of 'icon' itself, through the association with Diana, takes on yet more resonances, notably those of the indexical-democratic and of the spiritual.

The popular appropriation of 'icon' as taken from cultural studies also brings with it the 'indexical' inflexion of the sign that Williamson connects with democracy. The Burchill-Blair epithet of The People's Princess is of course a ludicrous impossibility in strictly political terms. But as a way of representing the significance of the Princess as it differentiated her from other members of the Royal Family, namely her similarity to 'us', it took hold of the popular imagination after her death. As with Williamson's description of the 'indexical' quality of the US presidency, the notion of 'People's Princess' also carried 'a measure of something' with its recognition of Diana's life as embodying approximations of the sort of democratic aspirations that Williamson suggests 'the "average person" can achieve' – and which appear quite independent of Diana as a royal personage.

The democratic impetus behind the popular endorsement of 'People's Princess' also affected the interpretation of the epithet

Diana herself had coined in the *Panorama* interview. Asked if she thought she would ever become Queen, Diana replied, 'I'd like to be a queen of people's hearts, in people's hearts, but I don't see myself being Queen of this country'. This answer had been translated into the much-derided figure, 'Queen of Hearts', source of much media punning and misogyny. But after Diana's death, the phrase was reinterpreted, reinvented almost, in public tributes that quite transcended the previous cynicism. 'Queen of Hearts' became 'Queen of All Our Hearts' in the messages to Diana, and now encompassed a range of hopes for some closer, more affectively democratic relationship between 'the people' and their royal 'representatives'. Lacking any overtly political momentum, such wishes have remained incipient and have so far, in a paradox of the consequences, served mainly to the rehabilitate and retrench the monarchy in a more 'Diana-like' direction.

The fact that the democratising potential implied in the Diana tributes has so far remained largely unrealised may also relate to the extent to which Diana was memorialised in so many other-worldly, spiritual terms. The religious aspect of Diana's iconic appeal had already been anticipated in commentaries during her life. Julie Burchill, for instance, notes: 'Far beyond being a Windsor, Diana has become an icon of sexy saintliness - the Church of England at play in high heels. She is Madonna crossed with Mother Teresa - a glorious totem of western ideals'.[36] And Camille Paglia predicts a key aspect of the mourning rituals when she describes Diana as 'a case study in the modern cult of celebrity and the way it stimulates atavistic religious emotions'.[37]

The emphasis on the caring and compassionate aspect of Diana's persona had, again, been subject to media ridicule and cynicism during her lifetime, as indicted by the savage deconstruction of The Healing Hands icon cited earlier. Yet after her death, the mounting piles of memorials offered a kind of ecumenical apotheosis of Diana. In a quite straightforward and unironic manner, tributes were offered on the lines of: 'Born a Lady. Died a Saint'; 'A New Angel in Heaven'; 'Princess of Love'; 'Like Jesus'. Without apology or embarrassment, routine reference was made to the heaped flowers as 'shrines' and the routes between them became those of 'pilgrimage'.

Thus the moment when 'icon' entered the vernacular was also when it re-acquired an earlier religious meaning. The concept of 'icon' meaning specifically 'the sacred likeness of the godhead' first entered the English lexicon through contact with Eastern - Byzantine - Christianity in the mid-thirteenth century, but was not in common usage until the nineteenth century.[38] In the twentieth century, the term becomes secularised in humanist studies and then routinised via journalism into everyday speech - as has happened with the routes of other numinous terms like 'aura' and 'charisma'. So, to summarise: through its association with Diana, 'icon' has accrued 'indexical' connotations of wished-for democracy and 'symbolic' connotations around celebrity, femininity and the contexts of cultural change. Finally though, with Diana's death and the entry into the vernacular, 'icon' embraces the numinous again. But at that point, probably all commentary, all analogy, all verbosity should cease: the level of the sacred is the truly ineffable.

(This article is based on a short contribution, 'Icon", for the Reports and Debates section of Screen, Vol. 39 (1) Spring 1998.)

## References

1   Nigel Fountain, 'A trash icon for our times' *The Observer*, 27 July 1997. p.21
2   Michel Foucault, *The History of Sexuality: Volume 1: An Introduction*, Allen Lane Penguin Books 1979. p. 33
3   Diana Simmonds, *Princess Di: The National Dish*, Pluto, 1984.
4   See also Celia Lury's exemplary account, 'A public romance: "The Charles and Di Story"' in L Pearce, J Stacey (eds), *Romance Revisited*, New York University Press, 1995, which, *inter alia*, discusses Diana's appeal to a 'global panhumanity' through a celebrity which blurs the public-private distinction and effects the 'symbolic castration' of Charles after 1983, confining him to a limited national and public role.
5   Simmonds, *Princess Di: The National Dish*, p. 66.
6   Simmonds, *Princess Di: The National Dish*, p. 111.
7   Simmonds, *Princess Di: The National Dish*, p. 108.
8   See also British *Vogue*'s tribute edition for the Princess, October, 1997, on how the magazine's make-overs and photo sessions contributed to Diana's continual celebrity transformations.
9   Simmonds, *Princess Di: The National Dish*, p. 108.
10  Andrew Morton's biography, *Diana, Her True Story*, Michael O'Mara Books, 1992, was the first detailed account of the Princess's eating disorders, the extent of her distress in a marriage which now appeared cynically arranged, and confirmed the existence of a mistress in Charles's life.
11  Rosalind Coward, 'The Royals', *Female Desire: Women's Sexuality Today*, Paladin, 1984, pp. 163-171.

12  Coward, 'The Royals', pp. 170-71.
13  Joan Smith, 'The Frog Princess', *Misogynies: Reflection on Myth and Malice*, Faber and Faber, 1989, pp. 54-64.
14  Smith, 'The Frog Princess', pp. 63-4.
15  Joan Smith, 'To Di For: The Queen of Broken Hearts', *Different for Girls: How Culture Creates Women*, Chatto and Windus, 1997, pp. 3 - 18.
16  It was widely believed at the time that Diana had collaborated in the Morton biography – although it was only revealed in the revised Foreword to the book, reissued in October 1997, that Diana was actually its main source.
17  Andrew Morton's sequel, *Diana, Her New Life*, was published by Michael O'Mara Books in 1994; Diana's *Panorama* interview with Martin Bashir was first aired on BBC-1, 20 November 1995 and then given worldwide coverage. In the interview, the Princess confirmed many of the incidents outlined in the Morton biographies and also acknowledged her own affair with the Guards officer, James Hewitt, thus, 'Yes I adored him. Yes I was in love with him. But I was very let down.'
18  Smith, 'To Di For', pp. 8; 10; 12.
19  Smith, 'To Di For', p. 11.
20  Beatrix Campbell, *Diana, Princess of Wales: How Sexual Politics Shook the Monarchy*, London, The Women's Press, 1998. Julie Burchill, *Diana*, London, Weidenfeld & Nicolson, 1998.
21  Julie Burchill, 'Di Hard: The Pop Princess', *Sex and Sensibility*, London, Grafton, 1992, pp. 233 - 244.
22  Burchill. 'Di Hard' p. 237
23  Burchill. 'Di Hard' p. 237-8
24  Burchill. 'Di Hard' p. 238
25  Burchill. 'Di Hard' p. 244
26  Burchill. *Sex and Sensibility* p. 11
27  Smith, *Different for Girls*. pp.x-xi
28  This essay first appeared in *New Republic*, 3 August, 1992 and was reprinted in Camille Paglia's collection, *Vamps and Tramps*, Harmondsworth: Penguin, 1994, pp. 163-171. *Diana Unclothed* was produced by Rapido TV for Channel Four and transmitted in the UK, 16 March 1993.
29  Paglia. 'Diana Regina' p.164
30  Paglia. 'Diana Regina' p.167
31  Paglia, 'Diana Regina' p. 170-171
32  'It is a point to remember that of all the ironies about Diana, perhaps the greatest was this: a girl given the name of the ancient goddess of hunting was, in the end, the most hunted person of the modern age' – Earl Spencer's funeral address, quoted in *Hello* tribute edition, 13 September, 1997.
33  See C S Peirce, *Collected Papers*, Harvard University Press, 1931- 58; and Peter Wollen, *Signs and Meaning in the Cinema*, Secker & Warburg,

1992 for an influential account of Peirce's work applied to film studies.

34   Reprinted in Judith Williamson, *Consuming Passions*, Marion Boyars, 1987. pp.75–90. This essay was first published in *Ten-8* in 1985.

35   Williamson, *Consuming Passions*. p. 76

36   Burchill, 'Di Hard' p. 243

37   Paglia, 'Diana Regina' p. 164

38   This is according to a lexicographer speaking on the Radio 4 programme *Word for Word* about the origin of contemporary terms. Transmitted on 31 August 1998, the programme chose 'icon' as the appropriate word to discuss on the first anniversary of Diana's death.

# 2. The Misfortunes of Virtue: Diana, the Press and the Politics of Emotion

## Scott Wilson

> *"Cover her face*
> *Mine eyes dazzle*
> *She died young".[1]*
> John Webster: 'The Duchess of Malfi' Act IV, Scene 2 (1623)

Nancy Banks-Smith's epigraph to her commentary on the television coverage of the death and funeral of the Princess of Wales draws an analogy with Jacobean tragedy. Like many other commentators, Banks-Smith notes the comparison even as she contributes to the media fictionalisation of the Princess's life. The Princess of Wales lived out a life of brilliant fictions;[2] the media not only told her story, it wrote and re-wrote that story according to a variety of familiar genres - fairy tale, romance, soap opera, morality play, tragedy and so on. The blanket coverage of Diana's life and death turned, essentially, on the suffering of a young woman whose beauty, frozen in the glare of camera flash bulbs, did not diminish. As Banks-Smith's quotation subtly suggests, this coverage involved both the endless, painful exposure to the rigours of popular narrative and the effacement of the real human suffering it produced. To the end, Diana's face was covered by the dazzling images that immortalised her.

At the same time as her death crystallised the iconic image of Diana, however, another image was withdrawn from media circulation: the image of the Princess, photographed by the paparazzi, dying in the crumpled Mercedes . Though the pictures were published in Germany, in Britain, a taboo was placed on those pictures of her dying moments, unconscious or in pain. They were subject to universal moral censure, deemed to constitute the very acme of intrusive prurience, the accursed part of the photo-archive, the dazzling, unbearable core of the story that must be covered over. In their place, the newspapers printed the image of the smashed Mercedes, a substitution that for some betrayed the same prurient impulse. The substitution seemed to imply that for the press, at some unconscious level, she *was* that crushed Mercedes. The edition of *Private Eye* that appeared on 1 September, the Monday after her death made the analogy explicit, as usual homing in on a perceived hypocrisy. It depicted an imaginary conversation between two outraged punters: 'The papers are a disgrace'. 'I know I couldn't buy one anywhere'. 'Here take mine, it's got a picture of the car'. This joke acutely locates censorious morality in the disappointed prurience that supports it. Already commanding a high price, the withdrawal of the pictures taken at the time of her death only heightened their value and desirability - and not just in simple economic terms. The British Sunday newspaper *The Observer* acknowledged the fascination the pictures would exert:

> 'These crash photos are likely to become under-the-counter cult objects - authentic snuff pictures and a repellent symbol of the amoral code of the tabloid photographers and the editors who profit from prurience'.[3]

This has not actually been the case, but *The Observer* is happy to enjoy the anticipation of its moral superiority over its peers. At the time, of course, this sentiment expressed a common view that these pictures do more than simply record a newsworthy event, a view that assumed, without fear of contradiction, that they contained something more prurient or obscene than those, for example, depicting the suffering of victims of war or famine. But it is no amoral code that has allowed countless intrusive photographs to be taken, sold, and reproduced across the world. The profit is gained from the very morality that, as with so many other pictures of the Royal Family taken incognito, likes to *see* in order to condemn, yet shakes its head at the image it has just bought. It is a *News of the World/ National Inquirer* morality whose sustenance depends on the objects of its

salacious disapproval. In this case, if the volubility of the condemnation is not simply the result of a disappointed moral prurience, then
it is because morality wishes to be protected from the destructive
reality of its own desire.

But in fact some of these 'snuff' images were indeed 'reproduced'
in the British press, on the day after her funeral, by the *Sunday Times*
in an article by the Insight team on Princess Diana's Last Hours.
The photographs were not reprinted, but they were described:

> *'One was a clear shot of her face, a hand stretched out as if*
> *reaching for Dodi. She looked superb, said Sola, she was*
> *still very, very beautiful and nothing suggested she would*
> *die a few hours later'.*

> *The Princess was unconscious. Her head was resting in the*
> *gap between the front seats. Her face was serene. There was*
> *just one bruise under her left eye. A trickle of blood ran*
> *down the side of her forehead'.*[4]

The pictures are recorded as described by one of the photographers,
the aptly named, to the British press, Romuald Rat, and Laurent
Sola, the agent who sold the pictures to the world's media shortly
after the crash, but withdrew them after her death some four hours
later. The images again betray the impulse to romanticise and
aestheticise Diana's life, even in her dying moments. Somehow,
inside the snarl of broken bodies and twisted metal, at the centre of
an infernal nightmare – 'and what could be more hellish than the
final image of the demon paparazzi swarming over the wreckage?'[5] –
a serene vision of beauty emerged to quell the inferno. In spite of the
moral execration thrown at the paparazzi, in spite of their obscenity,
their pictures apparently manage to preserve the beauty of the
Princess. That beauty is indestructible, indeed the single bruise and
trickle of blood merely serve to enhance it, even eroticise it.
Interestingly this myth of Diana's beauty intact amongst the appalling
wreckage of the crash is still being repeated and still retains its power.
Vicki Woods of the *Sunday Telegraph*, for example, recalled, on the
anniversary of Diana's death, her husband's account of the suppressed paparazzi images:

'My husband, having rolled off to work at four in the morning
on that Sunday a year ago, rang me from his newspaper office at

lunchtime to tell me that the paparazzi pictures had arrived on-screen. They'd been sent routinely, on the electronic browser, to Fleet Streets picture editors . . . He said: "Everybody's got them. Nobody will buy them. Not in England. Probably not in America. Maybe some German mag." And then he waited for me to ask what he knew I would ask, and said: "Slumped in the back seat as though she's fallen asleep. Everyone in the car looks horrific. Horrific. She looks beautiful. Her face is unmarked". He told me that everybody I could imagine had stood around the screen for a minute or two. Tired newspapermen in weekend clothes, who'd been up since three or four in the morning with blood on their hands – some of them had been up for 48 hours straight. They looked at the pictures with professional interest and some with agony. They didn't say: "O how vile, the ghouls, the vultures, how inhuman, what kind of lowlife could stand there snapping pictures?" They said: "Christ, she looks beautiful" and then they said: " Get rid of them". They were cleared from the screen'.[6]

The agony and the ecstasy: the professional equanimity of the tired hacks is broken by an epiphany of pure beauty among the horror, an image of beauty that even seems to redeem the hitherto lowlife paparazzi who stood round snapping. Even they are forgotten, or perhaps even forgiven. Yet hastily, they are erased, – 'get rid of them'. It is as if the newspapermen felt they were participating in a crime by even looking at them. The images apparently circulate in the virtual netherworld of the Internet, but most are fake. Nevertheless, they manage to preserve the Princess's bruised beauty, and the quasi-sacred eroticism it denotes.

It is the Princess's indestructible beauty, rather than the erotic *frisson* of its wounds, that discloses the truly Sadean nature of the press relationship with Diana. Like Sade's heroine Justine, in his novel *The Misfortunes of Virtue*, the sufferings of the Princess never diminish her beauty in the fictions written and reproduced by the media, never lead to the point where she is dismembered and destroyed. For Jacques Lacan, the object of Sadean torture is to retain the capacity of being an indestructible support:

*'Analysis shows clearly that the subject separates out a double of himself who is made inaccessible to destruction, so as to make it support what, borrowing a term from the realm of aesthetics, one cannot help calling the play of pain.*

*For the space in question is the same as that in which
aesthetic phenomena disport themselves, a space of freedom.
And the conjunction between the play of pain and the
phenomena of beauty is to be found there, though it is never
emphasised, for it is as if some taboo or other prevented it,
as if some prohibition were there.*[7]

As most acknowledge, the press construct an alternative, fictional
world in which celebrities and the wealthy disport themselves, a space
of imagined freedom. At the same time, this space also involves the
play of pain; it is filled with tears. In the case of Diana, this world
meant disappointment at the failure of the Wedding of the Century,
a loveless marriage to a cold and adulterous husband, loneliness,
eating disorders, suicide attempts, betrayal, and above all perhaps,
the constant intrusion of the chroniclers themselves who did not fail
to feature in their own tales. Throughout all the victimisation,
however, Diana's beauty remained indestructible, and even blos-
somed when she became not only the most celebrated female victim
of a brutal world[8], but the patron of victims everywhere: a friend for
life to the sick and hurting.[9]

In a Sadean manner, the grace and beauty of Diana functions to
support, that is maintain, sustain and even provoke, the spectacle of
suffering for our reading pleasure. She does not simply provide
imaginary protection from suffering; her own suffering, and the suffering she represents and comforts, she guarantees the truth of her
virtue, and indeed of virtue in general as it is popularly understood.
The truth of virtue, in this quintessentially modern, even Sadean,
sense, is established 'in the moving presentation of the victim or also
in every form of beauty that is too obvious, too present, so that it
leaves man speechless at the prospect of the image that is silhouetted
behind it and threatens it. But what precisely is the threat since it is
not the threat of destruction?[10] This 'darker image' is not just some
Gothic spectre, or demon paparazzo, threatening beauty's virtue with
destruction. The Sadean fantasm of tormented virtue functions
precisely to support a form of suffering that provides the signifier of
a limit: 'suffering is conceived of as a stasis which affirms that that
which is cannot return to the void from which it emerged'.[11] As
Lacan writes,

*'Here one encounters the limit that Christianity has erected
in the place of all other gods, a limit that takes the form of*

*the exemplary image which attracts to itself all the threads
of our desire, the image of the crucifixion.*[12]

There is no need to speculate upon J.G. Ballard's suggestion,
repeated at the time in the letters page of *The Guardian*, that if Christ
were alive today he'd die in a car crash. It is enough to note Diana's
connection with Mother Teresa (see Linda Woodhead's essay in this
volume), whose own demise five days after Diana's grounded the
connection in the uncanny, almost miraculous coincidence of their
deaths, which located Diana under the metaphor of saintliness. Her
sacrifice, then, situated Diana, or rather the beauty of Diana as the
suffering of suffering , as what is called in Lacanian theory, the *objet
petit à*, the object *in* desire. The *objet à*, for Lacan, is the good that
one pays for the satisfaction of one's desire.[13] It is this good. sacrificed
for desire, that, Lacan suggests, religion tries to recuperate:

> '*In a religious service, the flesh that is offered to God on the
> altar, the animal sacrifice or whatever, is consumed by the
> people of the religious community and usually simply by the
> priest; they are the ones who stuff themselves with it. The
> form is an exemplary one; but it is just as true of the saint,
> whose goal , in effect, is access to sublime desire and not at
> all his own desire, for the saint lives and pays for others.
> The essential element in saintliness resides in the fact that
> the saint consumes the price paid in the form of suffering'.*[14]

Two extreme points here link Diana, the People's Princess or Queen
of Hearts, to the *objet à*. For Lacan, the saint takes on, for the
collectivity, the question of existence and the desire of the Other
(the collectivity) in the visible suffering of his or her body, thus
sustaining and nourishing desire, the very desire of the collectivity, a
desire that is fundamentally death-driven. Second, the inert body of
Christ, or the saint, is thus incarnated, symbolically at least, into the
eucharist, the ritual of Christian consumption. In this way, Diana
applies a sacred gloss, or rather consecrates, all the products, artifacts
and relics sold in her name, turning the process of consumption -
such as queuing up to buy one's copy of *A Candle in the Wind* - into
a kind of ritual proper to the sublimation of desire in the symbolic
order. All the time, however, one is consuming Diana as *objet à*.

The same structure applies to secular as opposed to properly sacred beauty. Even secular beauty has been called 'the splendour of truth', but for Lacan,' it is obviously because truth is not pretty to look at that beauty is, if not its splendour, then its envelope'.[15] In this case, the unappetising truth enveloped by beauty is betrayed not only by the terrible reality of Diana's death and destruction, but also by the horrifying desire *for* that death and destruction implicit in the narrativisation of her tragic life. In the most public way, Diana gave up her life to the destiny of the signifier, and her image became the object of a mass desire. Focal point of a collective identification, her body bore the burden of a collective *jouissance* (an uncontrollable, sometimes ecstatic enjoyment associated with the spectacle of suffering). As Lacan continues, for Kant 'it is the form of the human body that is presented to us as the limit of the possibilities of the beautiful, as ideal *Erscheinen*. It once was, though it no longer is, a divine form. It is the cloak of all possible fantasms of human desire. The flowers of desire are contained in this vase whose contours we attempt to define'.[16]

But what happens when the vase breaks, when the support gives way? Interestingly, *The Sunday Times* Insight article also acknowledged, and to some degree furnished, a darker or more radical edge to desire by recording a contradictory account of the Princess's physical condition at the time of her death:

> '*Two of the nurses were physically sick when they saw her first, said a senior hospital source. They had been told she was coming in, and of course they often operate on crash victims. But seeing the most beautiful woman in the world lying on the operating theatre in that state was something they could never have been prepared for'.[17]*

It is not clear whether the state of the Princess was caused by the effects of the crash or the surgical attempts to save her life. Either way, the nurses' singular response was not caused merely by the familiar sight of a broken or destroyed body; 'they'd operated on crash victims before'. The nurses' excessive reaction, their involuntary revulsion, seems to have been produced by the sight of the 'real' body of Diana, the most beautiful woman in the world, the ultimate, most popular fantasm of desire, being opened up before their horrified gaze: her ribcage bared to general view, her heart physically manipulated by the surgeon.

As was evident, the vase could not contain the flowers which, in the wake of Diana's death, poured forth in an unaccountable excess that would not stop. The sickly scent of over a million fresh and rotting bouquets permeated Kensington and Westminster. The spectacle of consumption that surrounded the death of Diana was caught up, initially at least, with a nonidentical, general process of expenditure that, for many, had political implications. Or at least, it resembled the kind of expenditure that heralds radical political change. Martin Jacques, for example, called it a 'Floral Revolution'.[18] All the papers agreed that the violent emotions unleashed by the death had the potential to force epochal change.

While, for Diana, there may not have been a Lucius Junius Brutus to drive out the Tarquin dynasty from Rome, there was an Earl Spencer. As Matthew Engel wrote in *The Guardian*: 'This morning London is bracing itself for the Funeral of the Century. It is absurd to make comparisons with Victoria or George VI, or Churchill. The mood in the capital – intense, febrile, borderline irrational – has probably not been like this since the Gordon Riots, or the execution of Charles I'.[19] The next day, following Earl Spencer's 'electrifying' speech in Westminster Abbey, Engel had every reason to warm to his theme: 'If Earl Spencer had gone one step further and called for immediate insurrection, they would have marched'.[20] In the same issue, Anthony Barnett declared the Princess to be, retroactively and paradoxically, the first President of the Republic of Britain.

## II

How could such a sense of political crisis, surrounding the death and funeral of the Princess of Wales, develop so rapidly? How could such a banal and anodyne figure becomes its focus? Even if it was not evident at the time, it is now obvious that all this press fervour, excitement and speculation concerning imminent political change was nonsense. Nothing changed, or rather the *change* had already happened, and the public irritation with the irrelevant protocol of the Royal Family was merely symptomatic of that change. The change, however, had nothing to do with some kind of movement or progression from one political system to another: from monarchist to republican, say, or Conservative to New Labour, or from the politics of self-interest and greed to the new politics of caring and giving.

Rather, this change, it seems to me, has to do with a shift in the nature of history and the event, as it is popularly understood.

These days, history has barely anything to do with politics, in a traditional sense. However, history *does* have everything to do with the event as televised spectacle – that is, the event that is televised in the full sense of being arranged, organised and understood according to the logic and economy of the media image. This is to say, the event is not simply something that has appeared on TV; an event achieves its status as such, and even becomes historical, as a retroactive effect of the ratings it achieves and the volume of subsequent citations or sales of the image(s) it generates for other purposes (including those endless compilations of popular narrative). Diana's funeral, watched by an estimated 2.5 billion people around the globe, determined her death as an extraordinary historical event, even though its political meaning is negligible. A certain, highly *mediated* kind of popular or even democratic notion of the event and of history is being played out here, not only through the mechanism of the ratings war and the market. but also by the popular production of the televisual event evident in several forms; for instance, the fantastic display of flowers piled high in Kensington and Westminster, or the willingness of large numbers of people to *participate* in the production of a certain kind of televised spectacle either by queuing all night (as if for some important sporting event) to sign the books of condolence, or by turning a quasi-State funeral into a rock concert. I think Decca Aitkenhead of *The Guardian* was correct when she suggested that all the flowers and the queuing had nothing to do with grief. In her column, she wrote: ' Most of the millions are making this journey not in grief-stricken mourning for a woman they never knew, but from a desire to locate themselves in a spot where history will, for once, reach out to them . . . gathered together in a collective historic experience'.[21] Aitkenhead suggested that the small attempt made to shorten the queues or ameliorate the waiting was misguided: the longer queues were, the better people liked it because their length guaranteed the sense of an historic occasion. In itself, queuing for hours to sign one of the 43 books of condolence that no one will ever read demonstrates an acute awareness of history as archive; it also indicates the desire to record or rather bury one's trace in the archive of the event as established by the massed TV crews from around the world who came to film and interview the signatories.

However, while Decca Aitkenhead's column was admirably alive to the symbolic dimension of this great popular event, she was perhaps a little hasty in dismissing the imaginary register that was misrecognised as personal grief. After all, as so many attested, and as with so many other celebrities, we felt we knew her precisely because of the media narrative, because of the romance or soap opera or tragedy that we had bought. No doubt we were all, retrospectively, deeply affected by the pictures of Diana playing with her boys, the pictures that exuded the warm humanity of her image in contradistinction to the cold, grey formality of the other royals. Diana's self-proclaimed faults and foibles, her inadequacies, her alleged limited intelligence and so on made her an effective mirror for a million identifications. Some people even claimed to be more affected by Diana's death than by their own personal bereavements. It is clearly, therefore, quite incorrect to suggest that the emotion displayed was false or fake. And yet I would still suggest that though the tears were real, they did not correspond to grief. Perhaps the response to Diana's death approximated to grief, just as we could say that Diana's funeral approximated a state funeral, but fundamentally was no such thing. I am not quite sure *what* it was, but it was not a State funeral, nor was it designed to be, but was something else. Many who were there seemed to have been experienced it as a kind of black carnival; for those who consumed it at home, it was a great televisual event of a kind that uniquely binds the personal and emotional with the global-historical dimension at the level of a hyperfamiliar image.

It is nevertheless interesting to look at the close proximity between mourning and the popular, emotional response to this televisual event. There is a certain structure that might go some way to explain both the extraordinary grief that surrounded her death, and indeed the momentary sense of political crisis that accompanied it. Further, this structure could be described as peculiar to a general condition of postmodernity, or of global capitalism.

It is well known that any traumatic encounter with death may cause someone to reassess their own life, or life in general. God or paternal authorities supposed to safeguard the wellbeing of the community are frequently disclosed as impotent in the face of the death of a loved one, a terrible loss that seems to make no sense. In Lacanian terms, the 'real', in the form of an unsymbolisable excess, shatters the subjects imaginary integration with the symbolic order; this excess, manifested in experiences of horror, *jouissance*, abjection and so on – like the nurses confronted with the exposed body of the Princess – frequently produces more excess, expenditures of vomit, anguish, anger, violence, madness, (a million bouquets), until the subject is reintegrated into the normal ordered realm of symbolised reality. The anguish and violent expenditures disclosed by the lack in being demands, for Lacan, to be filled by meaning, by *logos*, in the form of the signifier of authority which reasserts itself, characteristically, in formal (i.e. empty) ritual. The process of mourning highlights the importance of symbolic rituals like funerals.

However, all this normally concerns personal grief. How can millions of people suffer grief simultaneously? How can the 2.5 billion who 'attended' her funeral, virtually, by way of the electronic media, mourn someone they had never met? What kind of subject do these billions constitute? What kind of ritual can reconcile them with the Other? Is it possible that they can have an Other in common? Of course there were some voices in Britain, barely heard, who risked public obloquy by declaiming that the world had gone mad. They were mostly (old) left-wing rationalists writing in the letters page of *The Guardian*, people who nostalgically maintain a rigorous distinction between image and reality, and are determined to remain sane. However, whether or not the world had gone collectively mad in early September 1997, for Lacan, there is a close link between mourning and psychosis. Both involve a questioning of symbolic authority, the truth or meaning of symbolised reality as it is commonly experienced and understood. In psychosis, the traumatic encounter with the 'real' can have other effects that are the inverse of mourning, producing not a reintegration of the subject and the Other but '*Verwerfung* (repudiation, foreclosure)'.[22] Foreclosed from the name-of-the-father, psychosis replaces a delusional metaphor that displaces, or functions in opposition to, the paternal metaphor, setting up another world alongside the one of conventional symbolised reality. Reality is replaced by simulation, say, the actual challenged by the virtual.'[23]

The strange canonisation of Diana, the saintliness with which she was endowed, and the consecration of consumption that followed in her wake, does not of course disclose a simple continuity with conventional religion – anymore than did Judge Schreber's belief that God wanted to make him his wife so that he could impregnate him and populate the world with lots of little Schreber's. Indeed, the mass idolatry of Diana, in its very proximity to, or simulation of, the conventional Christian structure, discloses a more radical shift than Schreber: it announces that the locus of celebrity has decisively replaced the locus of the sacred. The church *no longer has any meaning*; its rituals do not integrate traumatised subjects into its world of symbolised reality. This displacement, this radical shift, was never better exemplified than by the wave of applause that issued from the crowds outside Westminster Abbey during Diana's funeral service, and swept through the august congregation, turning it into a different kind of event entirely: a rock concert, perhaps, or maybe, people thought, hoped even, a political rally.

In Britain, no one was quite sure, in the midst of mass public mourning following Diana's death, whether the public reaction meant the death knell of monarchy or its Blairite modernisation. As the Press acknowledged, the funeral's unprecedented failure of decorum and protocol prevented the safe reintegration and reconciliation of British subjects with their monarch. Britain's relationship with its monarchy, it was supposed, would never be the same again. One way or another, then, Diana's death was seen to have brought the nation together – in grief, in rebellion or in some strange kind of worship – but in opposition to the symbolic paternal authority situated at the head of Church and state.

A little later, however, some noticed that this unifying effect had nothing to do with the traditional theme of narrating the nation at all, with or without the monarchy as its paternal metaphor. 'If there is any transcendental unifying theme,' wrote Linda Grant, 'a sense of Englishness, it is not an idea of nationhood but the image of Diana, crossing class and gender and racial and regional and even international boundaries – supranationalism.' [24] Other writers and newspapers underscored the theme and wrote of 'Globalised Evita',[25] or 'Diana, first lady of the global village'.[26] 'Bigger than OJ, Jackie or Nixon, Diana was bigger than the Royal Family, bigger than Britain, she was the world's'... and so on.[27] It became clear, in retrospect, that British subjects had already foreclosed their relationship with the Other in the form of traditional symbolic authority. Diana's death had already taken place in 'another world' than that of Britain: in the fictional world generated by the media, the current locus of collective identification and imaginary community.

With Diana's death, conventional forms of authority were spectacularly superseded, but this only made more visible the *moral* law already in operation in the mediatised West, and across large parts of the so-called globalised world of capital. This moral law has become identical to the law of the image that has no ground in anything other than death. From among the swarms of images produced by the great machines of the globalised media, Diana's death crystallised her image as a metaphor that cemented the law of the image in the real, authenticating a familiar kind of postmodern psychosis. This image becomes the pure form of a generalised economic mode, indifferent from and to anything else, unregulated by an order other than its own: an internally generated command of excess. Absorbing all signification and consuming any transcendental signifier that might impersonate external regulation, consumer capitalism knows no limits and no external master. Instead, the residual meanings that still cling to the image of Diana take on an inordinate power: those meanings coalesce around a maternal figure, a beautiful mother, who commands, with the full moral authority of her death that we have indirectly caused through the demands we made on her image, to assuage our guilt by giving to charity. The primary means by which we must give is to consume, to buy, in particular to buy Elton John's record 'Goodbye, England's Rose'. The very desire to consume the image of Diana has resulted in a gap, a pool of negative guilt, that has produced an even greater desire to consume her image, this time with the moral guarantee that it is for charity. Slavoj Zizek, discussing capitalism's loop of enjoyment, gathers together capitalism and hysteria in the vicious circle of desire, whose apparent satisfaction only widens the gap of its dissatisfaction. The connection, Zizek explains, indicates that

> '*It is against this background that we should grasp the logic of what Lacan calls the (discourse of the)* Master*: its role is precisely to introduce* balance, *to* regulate the excess. *Precapitalist societies were still able to dominate the structural imbalance proper to the superego insofar as their dominant discourse was that of the ancient Master. In his last works, Michel Foucault showed how the ancient Master embodied the ethics of self-mastery and just measure: the entire precapitalist ethics aimed to prevent the excess proper to the human libidinal economy from exploding. With capitalism, however, this function of the Master becomes suspended, and the vicious circle of the superego spins freely.*' [28]

The suspension of the function of the Master leaves the superego unanchored in the symbolic. The system of signification, no longer regulated by a master signifier, eschews structural imbalance to follow the rule of excess. In this situation, the superegoic moral law is a function of excess, demanding excess to feed itself and is therefore the accomplice, not the check, on an unrestricted amoral capitalism.

What are the political implications, particularly in Britain, of the emotionalism surrounding the death of the Princess of Wales? I have already noted that rationalist speakers, of the left and the right bemoaned the apparent sentimentality of the phenomenon, 'the elevation of feeling, image and spontaneity over reason, reality and restraint'.[29] This was not the case with Tony Blair and New Labour, however. Blair's performance and exploitation of the mass emotion was widely commented upon and admired. Some have been concerned at New Labour's apparent willingness to massage and exploit any emotive issue for the sake of political popularity, and were alarmed by Blair's astonishing public rebuke of Anthony O'Hear's essay 'Diana, Queen of Hearts' in the collection edited by Digby Anderson and Peter Muller, *Faking It: The Sentimentalisation of Modern Society*, a rebuke that seemed to confirm suspicions about Blair's use of popular emotionalism, fed and sustained by an aggressive media, as a means of prohibiting and repressing argument and dissent O'Hear's essay was certainly right-wing and even sentimental, in its own nostalgia for traditional forms of 'rank', 'duty' and 'protocol', but it did not warrant a denunciation by the Prime Minister to the press outside 10 Downing Street.

In a later essay in *The Guardian*, Decca Aitkenhead makes the connection between politics and emotional issues in a piece on how the heart rules the head in Nineties Britain, comparing mourners paying their respects to Diana with lynch mobs baying for the blood of newly-released paedophiles. Recalling that both Hitler and Stalin, like most dictators, were lavishly sentimental and liked weepie films (just as they liked genocide), Aitkenhead writes: 'Instead of congratulating the newly caring Britain and condemning the lynch mob, we should instead be examining what unites the two.'[30] She also mentions, in her final two paragraphs, how New Labour policy units have been doing research into the politics of emotion as a means of targeting not what voters think, but what they feel. There is also a Labour pressure group that has been set up to promote emotional literacy in politics. Aitkenhead makes the point, though she does not develop the idea, that both the volubility of public displays of emotion and its political exploitation is an effect of a post-ideological culture and the lack of a coherent

intellectual framework for politics. Certainly, emotion has been integral
to politics and political theory for as long as there has been politics. In
the modern era, it could be argued that the deployment of fear is central
to the Enlightenment's understanding of modern politics ,from
Machiavelli and Hobbes to the development of reforming and
revolutionary politics. The key issue is the shift in the object of fear
and loathing (and indeed from an object that is simply feared to one
that is feared *and* loathed). For Machiavelli the object to be feared is
the Prince himself, because it is the most efficient way of maintaining
order. However, there is the proviso that this fear must not turn into
hatred (through unjustifiable acts of tyranny), and the acknowledg-
ment that this fear (established through ruthless, but just punishment)
needs to be supplemented with a charisma that can be manufactured
by making it appear that *fortuna* (the People's Princess) is on your side.
With Hobbes, fear of the State of Nature needs to be transferred onto,
and transformed into, Awe for the Sovereign whose presence will hold
it at bay. But what lasts from Hobbes is the prior shift of fear onto the
neighbour: eventually, liberal politics is determined by fear of one's
neighbour (understood on the basis of one's own irrational and violent
nature, greed or passions and so on). Politics as determined by fear of
the Other, therefore, can work either as a unifying, universal principle
for economic liberalism, or a principle of opposition for class politics
(economic resentment, outrage, righteousness). In these terms, fascism
is a hybrid combination of Machiavellian and oppositional politics in
which the sovereignty and charisma of the leader is predicated upon
the radical heterogeneity (an abject loathing that has no rational basis)
of the object of fear; in the Nazis' case, the Jews (and a series of
subsidiary categories – communists, trade unionists, homosexuals,
gypsies, blacks and other races).[31] As the apex of a mass of
heterogeneous emotions and affections, the fascist leader functions as a
point of moral identification in which fear (established through moral
rigour and the ruthless suppression of base elements) certainly plays a
part. Notwithstanding Aitkenhead's association of New Labour's
emotional politics with Hitler and Stalin, I don't think that Blair is in
the fascist dictator bracket yet, nor do we seem to have an equivalent
for the Jews. I think what is intriguing about New Labour's interest in
emotional literacy is the intimation that emotions have to be read (and
to be read they need to be written). Perhaps there has been the tacit
realisation in some parts of Walworth Road that there need be no *object*
of opprobrium upon which to rise as the apex of heterogeneous

emotion, so long as there is a continuing narrative of shock, scandal, suffering and outrage to sustain a volatile, emotional electorate. The characters of these narratives need have no intrinsic quality or ontological weight (Jewishness), they just have to be unfortunate enough to get caught in the media's gaze. Aitkenhead mentions how the teenage nanny Louise Woodward became the object of mass emotion as, first, the innocent victim of hateful American employers and a foreign judiciary, and second as a greedy, inhuman childkiller (after she returned home complete with an American accent). The same effect is produced when an academic fails to go along with the ritual weeping over Diana: Blair has to speak. There is no empirical hate-object-victim, just a machine for producing and illuminating them.

Another aspect of New Labour's general populist strategy is of course its intimacy with certain areas of business consultancy. For a very long time, businesses have been making money by marketing their products through a direct recourse to emotions rather than information, assuming, no doubt correctly, that people do not consume rationally. It is also possible that sections of the population have become more emotionally volatile as an effect of the 'risk society', the rigours of a flexible workforce and the way traditional paternal structures break up or fail to provide a secure framework, emotionally or materially. The Henley Institute (linked with the think-tank Demos) recently showed, through polls, that Marks and Spencer is popularly deemed to be the most trustworthy British institution. Apparently, throughout the Eighties and Nineties, 'fluid zones of trust' have drained away from public institutions (the Church, education, police, civil service, Parliament) and are flowing towards major corporations that utilise, or indeed have a powerful influence over, the media and global modes of representation. The *modus operandi* of business corporations and political parties are moving closer together. It is, for instance, very often difficult to tell where New Labour's political strategy begins and its marketing strategy ends. Also relevant is the fact that marketing categories have replaced political classes; these are themselves based on the mass of data (for example, Sainsbury's Reward Scheme for loyal, that is regular, customers) which have been compiled by corporations on a population's consumer and lifestyle choices. Given all this, as well as the instantaneity of mass communications technology, it is easy to speculate how a political party might seek advantage through manipulating mass public emotions through new techniques that masquerade as 'extending the democratic process'.

In conclusion, then, we can see how Diana functioned to bind politics and economics together in, and as, a glittering media image that used the emotions aroused by the conjunction of beauty and suffering to sell pictures and magazines in unprecedented numbers. Rich, famous and beautiful, at once the epitome of extravagant global consumption and the finest flower of maternal feminine virtue, recognised across the globe for her fame, her beauty, her suffering and her charitable work, photographed in the arms of AIDS patients, in Pakistani hospitals, with victims of land mines in Angola and Bosnia, Diana provided a point of global identification through the spectacle of suffering. Indeed, Diana bore the burden of global desire precisely through the fantasy-scene of her own troubles. It is this configuration, it seems to me, that contributed to the massive affective response to her death. It is the kind of affectivity that would once have been attributed to literature, or links the tragic drama and the sentimental novel to the pornographic Sadean fantasy. That is why, on the question of the existence of the *one* sentient correlative of the moral law in its purity (acceding to moral law necessarily causes us pain, since it sets itself against our inclinations), Lacan believes that Kant is best illustrated by Sade's fictional constructions; where pain, 'the other's pain as well as the pain of the subject himself, for on occasions they are one and the same thing', is the horizon that must be breached in order for the floodgates of desire to open absolutely.[32] Diana, as a composite figure of glamorous excess (playgirl of the Western World) and friend for life to the sick and hurting, appeals to both a libertarian and a liberal conscience; her death broached the floodgates of desire, desire that manifested itself in an orgy of consumption ( 'Candle in the Wind' was already the biggest selling single of all time in Britain after it had been on sale for only 3 weeks).

Diana has become a powerfully maternal, superegoic figure who pins the politics of victimhood to the imperative to consume. While this paradox is not unknown - the proverbial superegoic puritan mother paradoxically inveighs her offspring to consume every scrap of their meal by reminding them of those less fortunate than themselves - it is remarkable how the spectacle of suffering celebrities, or celebrated suffering (Diana, Elton, Liz; Band Aid/Live Aid/A Candle in the Wind), has successfully impelled so many people to spend, spend, spend in order to save the world. In this sense, Diana is far from unique; this superegoic law precedes her and will no doubt continue when her image settles down to become merely another celebrity. Victim of victims in the pantheon of success, she urges us on, in death, to be what we 'wanna' be, do what we 'wanna' do, and in this way take on, metaphorically, the function of redeeming all the victims of the world. If it is true that, through its literary, or cinematic, modes of representation and interpellation, the globalised media enables the generalised foreclosure not only of conventional modes of political representation, but of any 'meaningful' relationship with culturally specific forms of symbolised reality, the aestheticised play of pain will continue to demarcate the limit between life and death, between the dead images of the media and those living outside the screen whose only means of realising themselves in, and as, a dead image is by purchasing one.

In the meantime Diana's cadaver lies interred in an airtight, 40 stone, lead-lined coffin.[33] The fantasy that 'age shall not wither her', nor the elements depreciate her beauty, has itself been vacuum-packed, held in reserve as if in the vault of some Swiss bank, guaranteeing the endless reproductions that circulate the globe.

# References

1  From John Webster, *The Duchess of Malfi*, cited by Nancy Banks-Smith in *The Guardian*, 8 September 1997, p.12
2  Brian Appleyard, *Sunday Times*, 7 September, 1997, 2, p.6
3  *The Observer*, 7 September 1997, p.19
4  *Sunday Times*, Insight, 'The Final Hours', 7 September 1997, p.15
5  Brian Appleyard, *Sunday Times*, 7 September 1997, section 4, p.6
6  Vicki Woods, 'Images of Diana', *Sunday Telegraph Magazine*, 30 August 1998, p. 9
7  Jacques Lacan, *The Ethics of Psychoanalysis*, London: Routledge, 1992, p.261,
8  *The Observer*, 7 September 1997, p.23
9  *Sunday Times*, 7 September 1997; p.19
10  Lacan, *The Ethics of Psychoanalysis*, p. 261
11  Ibid.
12  Ibid. p. 261-2
13  Ibid. p. 322
14  Ibid.
15  Ibid. p. 217
16  Ibid. p. 298
17  *Sunday Times*, 7 September 1997, p. 6

18   *The Observer*, 7 September 1997, p.12
19   *The Guardian*, 6 September 1997, p.1
20   *The Guardian*: 'She may be at peace. The nation is not', 8 September 1997 p. 1
21   Decca Aitkenhead, *The Guardian*, 5 September 1997, p. 17.
22   Lacan, 'Desire and the Interpretation of Desire in *Hamlet' Yale French Studies* 55/6 (1977) pp.11-56, 37-8
23   See Fred Botting on the close resemblance between this structure and the general condition of postmodernity in 'Culture, Subjectivity and the Real' in Barbara Adams and Stuart Allan (ed.) *Theorising Culture*, UCL Press, 1995. pp. 87-99.
24   Linda Grant, 'Englishness slips away'. *The Guardian*, 9 September 1997 p. 8
25   *The Guardian*, Leader, 3 September 1997. p.14
26   *Sunday Times*, 7 September 1997, p.6
27   *The Guardian*, 3 September 1997, p.6
28   Slavoj Zizek, *Tarrying with the Negative*, Durham, NC: Duke University Press, 1993 pp. 209-210.
29   Anthony O'Hear, "Diana, Queen of Hearts' in *Faking It: The Sentimentalisation of Modern Society*, ed. Digby Anderson and Peter Muller, Social Affairs Unit, 1998, p. 184
30   Decca Aitkenhead, G2, *The Guardian*, 16 July 1998, pp. 2-3.
31   See Georges Bataille, 'The Psychological Structure of Fascism' in Scott Wilson and Fred Botting (eds), *The Bataille Reader*, Oxford: Blackwell, 1997.
32   Lacan, *The Ethics of Psychoanalysis*, p. 80
33   See *The Times*, 6 September 1997

# 3. The Hollywoodisation of Diana

## Jeffrey Richards

Massive crowds lining the streets, mountains of floral tributes, hourly radio broadcasts retailing the nation's grief, a funeral attended by Hollywood stars, a two-minute silence, three women committing suicide out of grief – all these were features of the funeral of silent film star Rudolph Valentino who died suddenly at the age of 31 in 1926 at the height of his world-wide fame.[1] All these elements were repeated, except that it was two men who committed suicide, following the death at 36 of Princess Diana on 31 August 1997. For the death and funeral of Diana resembled far more the passing of a Hollywood star than a royal personage. It was all part of the Hollywoodisation of Diana, her transformation into a global superstar and the rewriting of her life to fit well-established cinematic paradigms of tragic royal romance.

The newspaper and magazine coverage of her life, the fascination with her clothes, her hairstyles, her holidays and latterly, her love affairs, were exactly the same as that accorded to Hollywood superstars. Like the great stars, Diana was both photogenic and charismatic. The camera loved her and she responded to it so well that her image became one of the best-known in the world. She also achieved the elusive blend of being both ordinary and extraordinary at the same time, which is often the secret of stardom. As a princess, a multi-millionairess and a jet-setting international celebrity, Diana was obviously extraordinary. But she was ordinary, too, in her humanity and vulnerability. The star with the tragic and troubled private life is often an identification figure for those whose own lives are beset by problems and unhappiness. This was part of the appeal of Marilyn Monroe and Judy Garland whose well-publicised health problems and marital misadventures, coupled with their early deaths, made them tragic heroines. It is no coincidence that Elton John's funeral anthem 'Goodbye England's Rose' was a reworking of a song originally about Marilyn Monroe. For Diana's stardom was of the tragic Monroe-Garland variety. Such stars live on in the popular memory when others who complete a normal span of years fade away.[2]

James Dean is a classic example. He had completed only three starring roles (in *East of Eden*, *Rebel Without A Cause*, and *Giant*) before he was killed in a car crash in his beloved Porsche at the age of 24 in 1955. But he became and remains a potent symbol for the young. The early death was an important element of the myth. So was his melancholy beauty: the sensitive boyish good looks, the sultry moodiness, the dreamy-eyed faraway look, actually the result of shortsightedness which compelled him to wear glasses off screen. He projected an intense vulnerability which teenage filmgoers found immediately appealing. He was in effect the first screen teenager, a term which had only just come into general use at that time. He patented the teenage uniform, which rapidly became obligatory in this country as well as America - blue jeans, white T-shirt, red windcheater - the teenage stance, the 'I don't give a damn' slouch, the cigarette permanently drooping from the corner of the mouth, the pouting 'drop dead' look. His films showed him coping with the perennial teenage problems of coming to terms with sexuality, establishing a working relationship with parents and trying to find a place in the world, all against a background of vague and generalised discontent with the family, authority and the *status quo*.[3]

Diana, too, had the beauty, the vulnerability and the early death. Her star image combined a number of classic archetypes simultaneously: the People's Princess, The Poor Little Rich Girl, the Secular Saint, the Single Mother/ Wronged Wife, the Tragic Cinderella, all of which have long Hollywood pedigrees. She was also - and this is something of a modern phenomenon - the real-life 'soap' star. As modern life has become steadily more privatised, and as for many people the insulated world of the private car, the owner-occupied house and the television have superceded the once dominant communal experiences of public transport, the cinema and the street, soap opera has come to replace real life as a source of gossip, attitudes and role models. The 'soaps' which are Britain's favourite television viewing, and American-influenced talk shows in which people parade their problems and bare their souls before openly partisan audiences, have conditioned the public's reactions to the trials and tribulations of others, both real and fictional. Some people seem unable to distinguish between the two. The Louise Woodward and O.J. Simpson cases are perfect examples of this new phenomenon of real life events which are treated, viewed and consumed as soap opera.

The British Royal Family has become a supreme example of the participatory 'soap'. Because through the media the public has shared the ups and downs, the joys and sorrows of this family, has taken sides and passed judgment as they would on characters in *Eastenders* or *The Archers*, they feel they know them personally. Sociologist Michael Billig discovered in his research into attitudes to the Royal Family that people familiarly referred to its members as Charles, Di, Philip, Fergie, Andy and the Queen Mum, as if they were characters in a long-running 'soap', though the Queen was always referred to as 'the Queen', for reasons to which I will return later.[4] Diana was the undoubted star of this 'super-soap'. Her eating disorders, suicide attempts, the broken marriage, the unhappy love affairs were all followed with the same eagerness and fascination that earlier generations of 'soap' fans had followed the fictional careers of Elsie Tanner and Meg Richardson. Some people came to feel that Diana, like other 'soap' heroines, was almost a member of their families, joining them in their living room via the television screen. Her celebrated 1995 *Panorama* interview, in which she bared her soul to the nation in intense closeup and with some carefully crafted lines ('There were three of us in that marriage, so it was a bit crowded'), was a classic instance of the blurring of the division between 'soap' conventions and real life.

After Diana's death, her home at Kensington Palace became an instant shrine, almost engulfed in flowers, candles and simple childlike poems attesting to the love felt for the dead Princess. It was almost a reversal to something pre-industrial, pre-modern, distinctly medieval. In the Middle Ages when a specially holy person, be it hermit or nun or princess, died, the people would gather spontaneously to lay flowers, light candles and create shrines. Then the Catholic Church, anxious not to allow uncontrolled cults to develop, would investigate the life, confirm its doctrinal orthodoxy and, once miracles had been performed, would canonise the dead person as a saint. During her lifetime, Diana had already become celebrated for another quasi-medieval phenomenon - touching for the King's Evil. As the anointed representatives of God on Earth, medieval monarchs in both France and England had magical healing powers, the ability by the laying on of hands to cure the disease of scrofula.[5] The last British monarch to exercise this power had been Queen Anne in the early 18th century. But Diana became a great advocate of hugging and touching the young and the sick. She earned great praise for embracing AIDS and leprosy sufferers, holding hands with the maimed and the dying, and while it may not have cured them, it was claimed that it brought them comfort and helped to change society's attitudes to such groups.

After her death, it was quite clear that another medieval phenomenon would grow up around her burial place - pilgrimage. It was an act of mythopoeic genius on the part of Earl Spencer to choose to bury his sister on an island in a lake on the family estate at Althorp. The idea of the Lady of the Lake and the related image of the body of Arthur, the Once and Future king, being rowed out to the isle of Avalon, completed the transformation of Diana into romantic legend. The estate and its specially-built museum of Diana memorabilia have already become a place of pilgrimage.

Pilgrimage to the shrine of Diana takes place for precisely the same reasons that pilgrimages took place in the Middle Ages to the shrines of Rome, Jerusalem and Compostella, and later to shrines at Walsingham and Lourdes.[6] There was the quest for sanctity, which is to be found by visiting the shrine of the saint. There is the desire to expiate guilt, in the case of Diana, guilt for buying the newspapers and magazines which stimulated the press hounding of her. There is the desire to be part of a like-minded group or community, in this case fellow-worshippers. There is the desire for a miracle cure; it must be only a matter of time before miracle cures are reported.

But Diana's resting place is not unique in becoming a place of pilgrimage. The tomb of rock star Jim Morrison in the Père Lachaise Cemetery, Paris, and Graceland, the Southern mansion that was the home of Elvis Presley, are regular sites of pilgrimage. Both Morrison and Presley died young. Both were stars. It is clear that for the modern, secular age, stars, particularly dead stars, have taken the place of saints, as objects of veneration.

An integral part of the pilgrimage phenomenon is the holy relic. Medieval pilgrims collected parts of the saints' bodies, objects which had been in contact with the bodies, images of the saints or badges that indicated they had visited the shrine. St. Thomas Aquinas said that such objects should be venerated both as physical reminders of the dead saint and as means of making spiritual contact with them. Since Diana's death a huge market in memorabilia has grown up, the latterday equivalents of relics, and court battles have been fought to copyright her name, her image and her signature.[7]

Not only was Diana a star in her own right, but her life was already being fictionalised before her death. In 1982, rival American television networks produced rose-tinted versions of the romance of Charles and Diana culminating in the fairytale wedding and the balcony kiss. Little known lookalikes played Charles and Diana. Real life stars played other real-life royals. *The Royal Romance of Charles and Diana* starred Dana Wynter as the Queen, Stewart Granger as Prince Philip and Olivia de Havilland as the Queen Mother. *Charles and Diana: A Royal Love Story* starred Margaret Tyzack as the Queen, Christopher Lee as Prince Philip and Mona Washbourne as the Queen Mother. Lee found his version 'terribly proper and ... unforgivably dull'.[8] But the blurring of soap and real-life continued. *Charles and Diana* included in its cast not just Margaret Tyzack, veteran of *The Forsyte Saga*, but in the role of Lord Mountbatten, David Langton, star of the long-running period 'soap', *Upstairs, Downstairs*. The part of Prince Andrew was played by Daniel Chatto, who in real life subsequently married the Queen's niece Lady Sarah Armstrong-Jones.

There was a fairytale quality to the way the romance was depicted: shy children's nanny, albeit from a wealthy aristocratic family, captures the heart of the heir to the throne and they appear to be ready to live happily ever after. The same ideas of fairytale underpin Andrew Morton's book *Diana: Her True Story*, the most influential publication in the whole Diana saga. Published in 1992, and as was revealed after her death, written with the full cooperation and participation of the Princess, it laid bare her unhappiness, her illnesses, the infidelity of her husband and the hollow sham the marriage had become. It created a sensation and led ultimately to the divorce, dividing the country and imperilling the monarchy. Morton deliberately constructs it as a fairytale gone wrong. Three times he refers to Diana as 'Cinderella'. Then, when he recounts the story of her 1983 Australian trip, he comments: 'She went out a girl, she returned home a woman', evoking the classic line in the musical *42nd Street* when stage producer Warner Baxter tells ingenue Ruby Keeler just before her debut: 'You are going out there a youngster but you've got to come back a star'.

Perhaps inevitably, Morton's book was turned into a three-hour television film *Diana: Her True Story* (1993) for Sky Television. It was billed as 'an intimate and heartrending account of the breakdown of the fairytale marriage between Prince Charles and Diana', and was smugly introduced by author Andrew Morton. Drably shot, cheaply produced and containing a gallery of truly appalling caricatures by otherwise reliable British actors, it ran through all the elements of the saga that had by now become familiar through the tabloid press: the marriage, the neglect of Diana, the bulimia and suicide attempts, the affair between Charles and Camilla Parker-Bowles, the separation and her building of a new life - all done without a spark of wit, originality or genuine emotion. But quality was not the point: book and film together helped transform reality into myth.

Within a month of the Princess's death, Martin Poll Productions, who had made this farrago, announced that they were planning a new film on the life and were beginning the search to find a leading actress to play Diana. In the event, they were beaten to the punch, with Channel Five Television showing, shortly before the first anniversary of her death, *The People's Princess*, a dramatised account of the last year of Diana's life, with Amy Clare Seccombe as Diana and George Jackos as Dodi Fayed. Written and directed by Gabrielle Beaumont, it was tabloid television, cheaply and opportunistically made, and was received with derision. Typically, Kate Saunders in *The Daily Telegraph* (17 August 1998) described it as a 'hagiography' and commented : 'For two hours actors rigid with embarrassment struck Madame Tussaud poses, and recited lines which could have been cuttings from *Hello*!... Its staggering vulgarity, seasoned with flashes of unintentional comedy, will make this the sort of thing played every Boxing Day by lovers of kitsch'. It is worth noting that before he became romantically involved with Princess Diana, Dodi Fayed was principally known for having produced the 1981 Oscar-winning film *Chariots of Fire* which celebrated the triumph of two outsiders in the 1924 Olympic Games; they were Scots Christian athlete Eric Liddell, who refuses to run on a Sunday and the English Jew Harold Abrahams who defies the amateur ethic by having a personal trainer, the Italian-Arab Sam Mussabini. *Chariots of Fire* damned the Old Establishment, headed by the Prince of Wales (the future King Edward VIII) and Lord Birkenhead as snobbish, racist and manipulative. It is a fascinating text when set against the battles of Dodi's father, Mohamed al-Fayed, with the contemporary British Establishment. However, even worse seemed to be promised with the announcement of a Broadway musical, *Queen of Hearts* by Stephen Stahl which would cover the breakdown of the fairytale marriage and end with Diana's death.

Its unique feature was that it cast Princess Grace of Monaco as Diana's Guardian Angel. The involvement of Princess Grace as a character reminds us that to some extent in the case of Diana, we have been here before. Long before there was Princess Diana, there was Princess Grace. The one was a princess who became a star; the other was a star who became a princess. The lives of both were imbued by the media with the aura of a fairytale. But in both cases the fairytale was soured by family scandals, and ended by death in a car crash.

Hollywood in its heyday had a fondness for poised, elegant, classically beautiful stars who could not act for toffee: Gene Tierney, Hedy Lamarr and Grace Kelly. Kelly achieved longer lasting fame than the other two partly because Alfred Hitchcock, who had a penchant for cool, classy blondes, elevated her to iconic status, coaxing from her performances that suggested a smouldering sexuality beneath the ladylike poise in the classic thrillers, *Rear Window*, *Dial M for Murder* and *To Catch a Thief*. But she turned cinematic fantasy into fact by marrying a European prince and making the ultimate transition from make-believe Hollywood royalty to the real thing. MGM, scenting box-office returns, cast her in an appropriate final film before her marriage and retirement from the screen; the studio dusted off a 1922 play by Ferenc Molnar first filmed in 1930 and refurbished it as *The Swan* (1956). Kelly was cast as Princess Alexandra of TransDanubia, beautiful but distant central European princess, whose mother is anxious to marry her off to Crown Prince Albert (Alec Guinness). It turned out to be a charming romantic comedy about the rituals and rigmaroles of a 19th century royal courtship, with an equally reluctant Princess and Crown Prince seeking to avoid the arranged marriage. Alexandra briefly falls for the handsome but humbly born tutor of her younger brothers (Louis Jourdan). But this temporary madness is dispelled and she settles for the understanding Crown Prince, who reminds her gently that such passions are not for royalty. This was the line frequently taken by Hollywood in its heyday, where duty was put before personal feelings and passion banished in films about royalty.

Grace Kelly appeared to live out this Hollywood philosophy when she married Prince Rainier of Monaco in 1956. She sought to play the role of Princess conscientiously. She bore Rainier three children, earned applause for her charitable activities with the Red Cross and sought to counteract Monaco's somewhat sleazy reputation by promoting cultural events such as an annual ballet festival. But she suffered three miscarriages and a difficult menopause, and she and Rainier drifted apart, apparently because of his jealousy of her domination of the headlines. Increasingly, they led separate lives, as she spent more and more time in Paris. There were a succession of young male companions, some platonic, some not. There were well-publicised scandals involving her daughter Caroline, whose unladylike conduct and unsatisfactory romantic attachments she found painful and embarrassing. But she maintained appearances right up until her death at 52 in a car crash in 1982. It was only after her death that a succession of books have revealed the truth of a profoundly sad and curiously hollow life.[9]

One of Diana's claims to fame is that she did not go along with the philosophy of keeping up appearances as Princess Grace had done. She was the product of a different culture, strongly influenced by the American practice which seems to have passed Grace by, of candid confession, seeking the inner self and therapy, the guiding principles of soaps and talk-shows. But if and when a full-blown Hollywood feature film is made of her life, it will be in a hallowed tradition. The lives and loves of the British Royal Family have been a staple of the film industry both here and in Hollywood for decades. Despite the fact that such films often reveal cruelty, immorality and ill-treatment within the Royal Family, their net effect is to strengthen and entrench the monarchy as they simultaneously mythologise and humanise it.

The cinema of monarchy has concentrated inevitably on the famous monarchs, the colourful, larger-than-life personalities, those whose exploits earned them nicknames and a place in popular folklore. In the heyday of Hollywood, even if the cinema audience knew no history, the mythic aspects of these monarchs would often be part of their cultural memory, if from no other source than school textbooks. Richard the Lionheart (Richard I), Bluff King

Hal (Henry VIII), Good Queen Bess (Elizabeth I), The Merry Monarch (Charles II), and Prinny (George IV) – these are the stars of history who all made it big on the silver screen, achieving portrayal by leading film actors. The less immediately colourful monarchs (Henry I, William III , George II) tend to languish in bit parts, if they manage to be seen at all. The story, probably apocryphal, that Sir Alexander Korda was inspired to produce *The Private Life of King Henry VIII* (1934) when he heard a taxi-driver singing the music hall song 'I'm 'Enery the Eighth, I am I am' illustrates the close link between popular folklore and the cinematic portrayal of royalty. It will be the folklore version of the Diana story, as constructed in the tabloid press, which will find its way onto the screen.

Some films have had the good grace to acknowledge the very tenuous link between their content and actual history. For instance, *The Prince and the Pauper* (1937), a swashbuckling romp which involves the 16th century child King Edward VI changing places with a beggar boy and eventually being restored to his throne by the intervention of Errol Flynn, prefaced its jolly proceedings with the statement: 'This is not history but a tale of once upon a time. It may have happened, it may not have happened. But it could have happened'. This motto should probably be attached to every so-called historical film dealing with the British monarchy. James Goldman, author of *The Lion in Winter* (1968), has also admitted: 'The film is only apparently historical, it is founded on the few facts we have but these reveal only the outcome of relation-ships. The content of these relationships, the people and their passions, while consistent with the facts, are my own invention.' The result, with King Henry II (Peter O'Toole), Queen Eleanor (Katharine Hepburn) and their warring sons locked up in a French castle during Christmas, 1183 and playing complex emotional games with each other, is a sort of Plantagenet version of *Who's Afraid of Virginia Woolf?*, another precedent the Diana film is likely to follow.

One way of achieving mythologisation is to cast famous screen stars as famous monarchs, for instance, Bette Davis as Elizabeth I, Charles Laughton as Henry VIII and Anna Neagle as Queen Victoria. These three stars became so identified with the roles that after initial appearances in the 1930s, they were called upon to repeat them in films of the 1950s. The charisma of the stars and the charisma of the monarchs commingle to elevate both the person and the role.

Mythologisation has also been accompanied and complemented by humanisation, but it is humanisation on the level of the historical romances of Jean Plaidy or Barbara Cartland. The presumed strong appeal to women of such royal romances is reflected in the fact that for every one film called *Alfred the Great*, there are half a dozen called *The Virgin Queen* or *Mary, Queen of Scots*, and that Charles II has been most frequently depicted in films dealing with his relationships with his mistresses (*Nell Gwynn*, *Forever Amber*, *Restoration*). The content of many of these films reflects what might be called the private life syndrome. They avoided concentration on real issues - social, political, economic, religious - which might cause controversy, invite censorship or affect profitability. Instead, they cater to the apparently insatiable desire of ordinary people to know about the personal behaviour of the great and famous. In so doing, they emphasise the very greatness of their subjects. For if they were not great, there would be no interest in their private lives. Thus *The Private Life of King Henry VIII* (1934) ignores the Reformation and concentrates on Henry's marital misadventures and *The Private Lives of Elizabeth and Essex* (1939) explores the unhappy love affair of the ageing Queen Elizabeth (Bette Davis) and her young favourite (Errol Flynn).

The cinema has shown a particular fondness for the great royal scandals of history, such as the love affair of Charles and Nell Gwynn (*Nell Gwynn*, 1934) or the clandestine 'marriage' of the Prince of Wales who later became King George IV and Mrs. Fitzherbert (*Mrs. Fitzherbert*, 1947). In each case, they end in tragedy with the woman ill-treated, abandoned or dead, and sometimes all three.

There are two films in particular which uncannily prefigure the Diana story as mythified by the media. *Mary of Scotland* (1936) starred Katharine Hepburn as Mary, Queen of Scots, Fredric March as James, Earl of Bothwell and Florence Eldridge as Queen Elizabeth I of England. As constructed by Hollywood's mythmakers, Mary is a decent, open-hearted, compassionate and loveable woman. She arrives in Scotland from France to take up the crown of her country, planning to govern with tolerance and sympathy for all. But she is scorned and undermined by an all-male Establishment led by her scheming and cruel-hearted half-brother, the Earl of Moray. She enters into a loveless marriage of state with Henry, Lord Darnley, but falls genuinely in love with the dashing and virile Earl of Bothwell. Throughout her reign, however, the cold and calculating Elizabeth of England plots against her. High politics eventually come between Mary and her Bothwell. He dies half-mad in a Danish prison, and after years of imprisonment in England, Mary is beheaded at the orders of Elizabeth.

There were even closer parallels in *Saraband for Dead Lovers* (1948) a British film which centres on the ambitions of the Hanoverian dynasty to secure the succession to the English throne, which they finally achieve in 1714. Beautiful, innocent and romantic Princess Sophie Dorothea of Celle (Joan Greenwood) is married off for reasons of state to the gross and unfeeling George Louis (Peter Bull) (the future King George I), son of the Elector Ernest Augustus of Hanover. George Louis rapes his wife on their wedding night, casually sends his brother to his death on a hopeless military expedition, flaunts his mistresses, and is bored by his children. Despairing of her loveless marriage, Sophie Dorothea embarks on a love affair with the handsome and dashing Count Königsmarck (Stewart Granger). But the affair is discovered, Königsmarck is killed and Sophie Dorothea is immured for life in a distant fortress. The entire Hanoverian royal family are shown as cold, calculating and cruel, even the Electress Sophia (Françoise Rosay) who has suppressed all emotion, tolerated her husband's infidelities and focused all her energies on gaining the English throne for her son.

The great friendships of monarchs similarly end in estrangement and death for the friend, as in *Beau Brummell* (1954), *Becket* (1964), *A Man for All Seasons* (1966) and *Mrs Brown* (1997), starring respectively Peter Ustinov as the future King George IV and Stewart Granger in the title role, Peter O'Toole as Henry II and Richard Burton as Thomas Becket, Robert Shaw as Henry VIII and Paul Scofield as Sir Thomas More, and Judi Dench as Queen Victoria with Billy Connolly as her favourite ghillie John Brown.

The moral of these films is clearly enunciated by Electress Sophia, mother of George I, in *Saraband for Dead Lovers*: 'Royalty may not look for happiness such as others may find'. The implicit assumption behind all these films is that being royal does not make you happy, and the job of ruling should be left to people who have been trained to endure the unhappiness. This is a similar idea to the argument that having money is no guarantee of happiness. I have long regarded this as a fiction put about by the rich to stop people wanting money. The 'unhappy royalty' idea similarly serves to discourage people from wanting power. Unhappiness is the price of privilege.

The setting of the films confirms the distance of the royal stars from the reality of the ordinary spectator. At least two royal films (*Tower of London* and *The Lion in Winter*) take place almost entirely within the confines of royal castles. Most other royal films involve their characters spending much time in castles, palaces and country houses. So, whatever personal traumas the royal personages undergo, they remain above and beyond ordinary men and women. They are a race apart, special beings whose lives and loves we, the lesser mortals, are privileged to glimpse. So humanisation and mythologisation take place, but within a framework which reinforces the elevated status of royalty.

The doctrine which this dual cinematic approach most recalls to mind is the old medieval doctrine of the 'King's Two Bodies'. This theory held that the King had two bodies, his human body which lived and died and was subject to human frailties, and his royal body which coexisted with it, representing his kingly role, and which never died. Hence the royal salutation: 'The King is dead. Long live the King'. This doctrine was extremely useful, for it could excuse bad deeds done by the monarch (attributing them to the human body) without denying the validity of monarchy (which remains sacrosanct in the royal body). So it is with cinema and its portrayal of Henry VIII, Charles II , and George IV, whose personal peccadilloes in no way tarnish the idea of monarchy. When there is occasionally a really bad king, he is a usurper who has set aside the legally and divinely ordained order of succession and has to be disposed of to make way for the rightful monarch. This is particularly true of the four major films dealing with Richard : *Tower of London* (1939) with Basil Rathbone, *Richard III* (1956) with Laurence Olivier, *Tower of London* (1962) with Vincent Price and *Richard III* (1995) with Ian McKellen. All four end with the death of the usurper, and the advent of an idealised Henry VII, who reaffirms the strength of the monarchy.

The cinematic cycles of royal films tend to be tied to events within the British Royal Family itself. For instance, the 1937 version of *The Prince and the Pauper* carefully included a lengthy coronation sequence to cash in on interest created by the coronation of George VI on 12 May of that year, and the films *Young Bess*, about the unhappy love of Queen Elizabeth I for Thomas Seymour, and *The Sword and the Rose* about the more successful romance of Princess Mary Tudor and Charles Brandon, were produced in anticipation of the coronation of Elizabeth II and released in July 1953, the month after the real-life event on 2 June. Until very recently it was not possible to depict living people in films. The censors forbade it. But the relaxation in censorship and the greater irreverence in society at large has ended that prohibition.

The latest cycle of royal films has been the product of the marriage and divorce of Charles and Diana. But it is films about other royals during the cycle that have perfectly illustrated the humanisation and mythologisation technique at its best. These are the film versions of hit plays by Alan Bennett, *The Madness of George III* (filmed as *The Madness of King George*) and *Single Spies* (filmed as *A Question of Attribution*). They featured award-winning performances by Nigel Hawthorne as King George III and Prunella Scales as Queen Elizabeth II. Both succeeded in evoking considerable sympathy for monarchs facing up to betrayal, conspiracy and political pressure. The manner of Diana's death and the reaction to it ensures that all the ingredients are in place for the classic cinematic tragic royal romance – *Saraband for Dead Lovers II*. But like all its predecessors, it is likely to confirm the ingrained royalism of the British people which the cinema has done so much to sustain over the past fifty years.

Tony Blair, who caught the mood of the nation so well in the days following the death, dubbed her 'The People's Princess'. The term has come to be overused – the People's Lottery, the People's Europe, the People's Dome, even the People's Champion, Alex Higgins, the snooker player. But in the case of Diana, it had a point. When Earl Spencer said in his memorable funeral oration that Diana did not need a royal title to do what she did, he was mistaken. Had she not married the Prince of Wales, no one would ever have heard of her. She would have lived and died in obscurity, probably as an upper class wife and mother in the Home Counties. The fact that she was a Princess is of the greatest significance. At the time of the wedding of Charles and Diana, public approval of the monarchy was running at about 80% of the population. There were calls for the Queen to abdicate in favour of the young couple but, mercifully, these calls went unheeded. Yet it had been a fairytale wedding and the British love their fairytales. Part of the bitterness felt by many about the divorce was dismay at the destruction of their fairytale.

This was compounded only a year later by the tragic death of the fairytale princess. The unforgiving attitude displayed by the public towards Camilla Parker-Bowles derives from the fact that she has been cast in the role of the wicked witch who broke up the fairytale romance.

On the day after the funeral, the 'heavy' Sunday papers such as *The Independent* and *The Observer* claimed that the end of the monarchy was at hand and their longed-for republic was imminent.[10] This was hysterical nonsense. The funeral and the grieving were a profoundly royalist phenomenon. In opinion polls carried out the week after the funeral, support for the monarchy had risen to about 70%.[11] Since the advent of opinion polls, there has never been more than 20% in favour of a republic, and that has not altered. What was worrying for the monarchy was the decline in the personal popularity of Prince Charles during the prolonged period of conflict with Diana, and calls for the monarchy to skip a generation and go directly to Prince William. The fact that a third of the population were prepared to contemplate a teenage boy as King is further evidence of deepseated royalist sentiment. But since the funeral, Charles' stock has steadily risen. A poll taken on the first anniversary of Diana's death recorded 75% in favour of monarchy and 61% in favour of Charles succeeding to the throne in due course.[12]

Britain is a royalist country because the monarchy is the symbol of the nation. Where other countries' national anthems celebrate the fatherland or the flag, the British national anthem is 'God Save the Queen'. It is because the Queen is the embodiment of Britishness, that she was viewed rather differently from the other members of the royal soap opera by Michael Billig's research respondents. Criticism of the monarchy, therefore, is in part a case of the nation criticising itself, just as it celebrated itself at the time of the coronation in 1953 and the Queen's Silver Jubilee in 1977. Even without Diana, the monarchy would have needed to change. It remains very largely an imperial monarchy in a post-imperial age. The Diana divorce crisis brought to a head the debate which had been welling up about the nature of the monarchy. The Queen recognised the need to adapt if the institution was to survive. She agreed to pay income tax, to prune the Civil List and to open Buckingham Palace to the public. Diana's role in all this was to develop a new style towards the performance of royal duty, an openly emotional, visibly caring, populist and clearly compassionate style. In the prolonged and often bitter and demeaning period of the marriage breakdown, some shortsighted commentators claimed she was out to destroy the monarchy. When confronted with that charge in her *Panorama* interview of 1995 she flatly denied it, pointing out that the Crown was her son's heritage and she was carefully and comprehensively training Prince William to be King and to undertake the duties in her new style. Part of the grief for Diana will have lain in the recognition that someone who was helping to change the nature of the monarchy, and thereby of British identity, had been lost. The fact that the people took her at her own valuation and grieved for her as 'The Queen of Hearts' is evidenced by the large number of giant playing cards that appeared at the various sites of mourning. The fact that it has been used for the title of a Broadway musical brings us back to the point that Diana, mythologised in life and death, remains a star, and her star status reinforces and strengthens the system of monarchy.

# References

1   David Birt, *Valentino: a Dream of Desire*, London: Robson Books, 1998.
2   Richard Dyer, *Stars*, London: BFI Books, 1979.
3   Paul Alexander, *James Dean: Boulevard of Broken Dreams*, London: Little Brown, 1994.
4   Michael Billig, *Talking About the Royal Family*, London: Routledge, 1992.
5   Marc Bloch, *The Royal Touch*, London: Routledge, 1973.
6   Jonathan Sumption, *Pilgrimage*, London: Faber, 1975.
7   BBC-1 *Panorama* 18 May 1998, *The Diana Dividend*.
8   Christopher Lee, *Tall, Dark and Gruesome*, London: Victor Gollancz, 1997, p.266.
9   Robert Lacey, *Grace*, London: Sidgwick and Jackson, 1994.
10  See for instance *The Observer* 7 September 1997: 'The institution can stagger on but ...it is clear the end is approaching'.
11  Gallup Poll (*Daily Telegraph* 11 September 1997) found 71% in favour of the monarchy and 11% for a republic; Mori (*The Sun*, 9 September 1997) found 73% supporting the monarchy and 18% for a republic. But 31% wanted the Queen to step down immediately in favour of Prince William. ICM (*The Observer* 14 September 1997) found 74% in favour of monarchy and 12% for a republic with 53% wanting the crown to pass directly to Prince William.
12  MORI (*Mail on Sunday*, August 23, 1998) found 75% favouring the monarchy, 16% a republic. But belief that Prince Charles should succeed and would make a good king had risen from 42% at the time of the funeral to 61%.

# 4. Diana Al-Fayed: Ethnic Marketing and the End(s) of Racism

**Emily Lomax**

## Muslim Diana, Shock

And what if there had been no crash? What if, as princesses are supposed to, she had lived happily ever after? Married to Dodi, a Muslim convert like her friend Jemima Khan, with a new generation of glamorous Muslim children becoming *Hello!* celebrities in their own right, what would have been the future for Diana?

With the wealth of her new family behind her, and a father-in-law with his own axe to grind, his own press machine and a desire for publicity to rival her own, Diana Al-Fayed would have remained well-equipped to continue her war of words with her former husband. It is quite possible that she would have continued her campaign to discredit him and , as she did in the famous *Panorama* interview of 1995, promote her son's preferment to the throne. One can only speculate how the Royal Family anticipated this prospect, how they might have coped with the perceived alien vulgarity of the new wing of their extended family. As Leslie White of *The Sunday Times* writes:

> '*Imagine it. Lady Diana of St Tropez and Knightsbridge, yachts, jet skis, Hollywood glitter, a handsome husband, and charity causes underwritten by an indulgent father-in-law . . . But while most of us were smiling at her good fortune, upper-crust stomachs were churning on the grouse moors – to think of that parvenu shop-keeper, Mohamed Al-Fayed, who would have to become British, playing grandad to the future king.*'[1]

For Salman Rushdie, Diana's love for Dodi Fayed must have felt to his father 'like a moment of sweet triumph over the establishment. Diana alive was the ultimate trophy'.[2] The Princess was the jewel in a considerable crown of British collectables: Harrods, a tranche of Conservative MPs, Fulham Football Club and the Estate of the Duke and Duchess of Windsor, yet still the Establishment would not grant him the British citizenship he desired. Denied membership to Britain in the normal or official way, Mohamed Al-Fayed seemed intent on buying up the country, or at least its prize possessions. This sense of Britain's 'family jewels' being stolen, or falling into the wrong hands, has of course increased since the blame for Diana's death has shifted from the paparazzi to the alleged recklessness of the Fayeds and their drunken driver, Henri Paul.[3] This sentiment was brutally pre-empted by Camille Paglia, at the time of Diana's death, when she did not hesitate to regret the fatal 'misjudgment' that entrusted Diana's life and safety 'to this scumbag Dodi Fayed and the people around him who are all incompetent idiots'.[4] This vituperation continued with the publication of Tom Bower's biography of Mohamed Al-Fayed.[5] Discussing the book and his own dealings with Al-Fayed as London editor of *Vanity Fair*, Henry Porter calls him a vindictive, sexually-obsessed bully who routinely sexually harassed the female staff of Harrods.[6] Reviewing the book in *The Guardian*, A.N. Wilson continued the theme of alleged bullying cruelty, obscenity and sexual predation, calling Al-Fayed an illiterate 'scumbag' and a 'Satanic little creep'.[7]

While for some, then, the Princess of Wales' association with the Fayed family contributed to her death, for others that death provided a liberation from their crass clutches. Julie Burchill, characteristically, viewed a sleazy future of indulgence, neglect and ultimate abandonment for Diana Spencer: 'Lady Diana Al Fayed, an Arab merchant's bit of posh, endlessly sunning herself on the deck of some gin palace hooked up in the Med., toasting herself until her skin lost its bloom and she lost her husband to a newer model.'[8] The implicit racism betrayed by the snobbish view of the Fayeds as *parvenu* shopkeepers, Arab merchants, scumbags and incompetents, is confirmed in the view that Diana's death in Paris was almost a blessed release from a fate worse than death: the appalling vista of the classy image of Diana as England's rose, this precious and beautiful icon of Englishness, becoming soiled in the hands of scummy, vulgar Arab *parvenus*. Burchill emphasises the whiteness of Diana's skin as an object of desire for Dodi, implying that when her skin aged and darkened in the sun, he would be off like the voracious black man that he was, in search of new, pale northern European flesh. This is an emphasis reiterated by A.N.Wilson when he writes of Mohamed Al-Fayed's predatory taste for tall, blonde, provincial English girls that culminated in his successful courting of the Princess of Wales for his son.[9] There is no question, then, that criticism of the Fayeds is deeply racialised, that it predates Diana Spencer's association with the family, and is of course tied to general resentment towards Arabs and western orientals with wealth. An article in a *Private Eye* collection, for example, prefigures uncannily the connection between the Fayeds and the Windsors, with the self-proclaimed anti-Establishment magazine hysterically lampooning the thought that the two should come together. In a satirical 'Court Circular', the Queen meets 'King Faht of Saudi Arabia', the 'Richest Wog in the World' and forms a procession to Buckingham Palace that includes HRH Mohamed Al-Fayed, Keeper of the Harrods, Crown Prince Mamoun al-Portakabina, His Royal Excellency Prince Mahmoud Cashandcarry-El-Binliner, Minister of Money, His Royal Excellency Al-an Koran, assorted camels, various Mercedes and so on.[10] What is very characteristic about this is that the racism is couched in snobbish irony, 'another pleasurable way of expressing the thought' as Freud noted,[11] that disingenuously constructs a 'knowing' relationship between the magazine and its predominantly white readership, apparently beyond racism, even though the very enjoyment of the joke depends on a complicit racism to begin with. Any attempt to critique such appropriations of racist discourse can then be dismissed as at best humourless, or even containing their own racist fantasy within the deliberate misinterpretation of the joke.[12]

Alongside the racist fantasies, a variety of questions, and speculations - constitutional, political and cultural - surrounded the prospect of Diana Spencer's betrothal to 'the Egyptian playboy' Dodi Fayed. These speculations of course concerned the nature of her relationship with the Fayed family, her plans for marriage and for raising another family, indeed her possible pregnancy at the time of her death. Further, there were speculations about her interest in Islam and, related to this, her friendship with Jemima and Imran Khan. Though no longer a cricketing hero, Imran Khan remains a glamorous figure in or out of white flannels. Public School and

Oxbridge educated, classically handsome, Khan could be a character out of a Mills and Boon romantic fantasy resonating with imperial nostalgia of passion in 'The Far Pavilions'. With his entry onto the Pakistani political scene, however, Khan has become a more ambivalent figure, attracting suspicion both with his public promotion of Islam and his claims about racism in English cricket (provoked by repeated accusations on the part of English cricketers about Pakistani bowlers' cheating and ball tampering) that resulted in a celebrated trial and successful defence against claims of libel brought by former England cricketers Ian Botham and Allan Lamb. In his stand off against Botham in particular, characterised as the essence of orthodox English masculinity,[13] Khan became the focus of intense popular hostility. At that point, he was no longer the romantic buttress of nostalgic Englishness in his position within the game of cricket-as-gift-to-the-Empire, but became an aggressive and resentful outsider. Mike Selvey recalled the racism that spilled over in the reporting of the trial, and how in parks and on cricket fields all over Britain, Pakistani cricketers – schoolboys and men – became the targets of crass sniggers and insinuations about being cheats and ball doctors.[14]

Along with popular unease about the Princess of Wales' association with Pakistanis, the prospect of a marriage with Dodi Fayed raised serious constitutional questions concerning the religious integrity of the Royal Family, and more particularly the second and third heirs to the throne, William and Harry.[15] Given his parents' eclectic approach to matters of religion, could the faith of the future King William V be adequately defended in a volatile international scene increasingly riven along religious and ethnic grounds? Prince Charles' comment that he wished to become 'Defender of Faiths', rather than just 'Defender of the (Protestant) Faith' was, however clumsy, a symptom of the persistent debate about the Disestablishment of the Church of England and the appropriateness and relevance of the monarchy's ties with one branch of one religion in a multicultural society. Certainly the press in parts of the Muslim world commented with force upon this; reports of Diana's imminent conversion were to be read in the Egyptian press, and an article attributed to Imran Khan read:

> *'The death of Lady Diana was very touching and was felt*
> *by all races and religions. As far as I would like to comment*

*on the subject, she had a great interest and admiration for
the religion of Islam. She would always be inquisitive about
it. After my marriage to Jemima she saw the wonders of
Islam and how it had reformed Haiqa. As I hope, it has
made the world realise that marriage to Dodi was not to be
by the grace of Allah. Maybe it would have been a huge
threat to the West of Lady Diana reverting to Islam, or
even carrying an Islamic name, as she would still have been
a mother of a future king. Only Allah knows the Truth, but
. . . the probability of Lady Diana reverting were excellent.*[16]

Whether this statement is by Imran Khan, or taken from comments
made by him, is unverifiable, but it is a fairly uncontroversial account
of many people's views in the Islamic world and elsewhere. For
example, Imran Khan's mother-in-law, Lady Annabel Goldsmith,
recalled in *The Daily Mail* Diana's expressed interest in the religion
during time spent with her in Pakistan, and how Diana received a
copy of the Qur'an from her houseboy.[17]

Perhaps Diana Spencer's interest in Islam is another instance of
what Paul Heelas, in this volume, calls her 'spiritual shopping', in
which a variety of ethnic spiritual goods could be purchased, along
with other accessories, as part of this year's look, a kind of Islamic or
Asian chic.[18] But perhaps there was more to this interest in other
cultures, spiritual or otherwise. There is certainly a story to be told,
one way or another, of the events of Diana's last years and of the
development and publicising of that interest. In the final year of her
life, she was photographed with a Hindu *bindi* visiting a temple in
Neasden; during the time when her friendship with the Khans
seemed to deepen she visited, accompanied by great publicity, the
Shaukat Khanum Memorial Cancer Hospital in Lahore, and was
frequently photographed attending fundraising functions for the
hospital back in London in a designer *shalwar kameez*. Less
welcomed, perhaps, was the publicity surrounding her friendships
with a string of Asian men, although not all of them were Muslim,
before her involvement with Dodi Fayed. These included mil-
lionaire Guli Lalvani and Dr Hasnat Khan, whose parents she called
on in secret when visiting the Jemima and Imran Khan in Pakistan.
This publicity reportedly infuriated Dr. Khan so much that he ended
the relationship. His friend told *The Daily Mirror* that there were

'problems over his religious background. Although Diana has become fascinated by the Muslim faith, his family would expect him to undertake an arranged marriage, and that would be impossible in this case.'[19]

Whether or not these connections were part of a pattern of spiritual shopping, accessories to her exotic narcissism, it may be possible to suggest that they nevertheless located Diana as a focus of British Muslim, particularly British Asian, identification. After her death, a vigil was held by Muslims in Southall throughout her funeral, and *The Observer* reported the emotional reactions to Diana's death of British Muslims present at London's Central Mosque on the day of her funeral:

> '*In the mosque, Muslims had been praying for Diana all morning. Mr K.M. Iqbal said: "I think many Muslims would have been pleased if Diana had married Dodi Fayed. The only positive thing to come out of this tragedy is that it has brought a greater understanding between Muslims and Christians . . . Many at the mosque hoped the hearse would stop outside and rumours that it would spread quickly through the crowd. But as the convoy sped past, many wept. Mrs Nagy simply repeated: 'It didn't stop, it didn't stop'".*'[20]

Others even felt that Diana's relationship with Dodi had the potential to herald an era of religious tolerance and co-existence, locating its romance in the idea that her active interest in other faiths would function as a general fillip for multiculturalism, and that it would be welcomed by Muslims as a symbolic invitation to participate fully in Western society. Theodore Zeldin wrote:

> '*The culture of intimacy attempts to achieve what international power politics cannot; it is all about the crossing of frontiers ... it is a tragedy that Diana has not lived to pursue her friendship with Dodi Fayed, whom the Arab world has made its hero. They bridge the gap between two forms of intimacy. Eliminating the mistrust between Islamic and Western Civilisation requires the multiplication of personal friendships, the establishment of emotional bonds, as much as political generosity*'.[21]

As part of this imagined *détente* between East and West, the press did not fail to draw the connection between the arranged or dynastic marriage of Charles and Diana (and its subsequent difficulties) and the well-publicised problems experienced by some 'westernised' British Asians whose marriages are arranged for them by their parents. It is difficult, though, to give much credence to a sense of shared experience between English aristocrats undergoing the intense pomp and circumstance of a Royal Wedding and second and third generation British Asians struggling to align cultural pressures of their own with their families' expectations and heritage.

The Press xenophobia and racism directed at the Fayeds, the Establishment anxieties about the religious and constitutional integrity of the institution of the Royal Family, and the popular romantic (equally liberal secular, Christian and Muslim) sympathy for the romance between Diana and Dodi, the man with whom she would finally find happiness – all these elements shook public confidence in the Windsors, raised suspicions about official attitudes to Diana and helped fuel the inevitable conspiracy theories. These began almost immediately after the crash and have proliferated on the Internet ever since, providing much of the material for newspaper articles and television documentaries in the following year. Though theories on the World Wide Web constructed a range of suspects, from the British and French security services to the Pope, the vast majority concerned the British Establishment's relationship to the Fayeds, and the presumed horror that an Islamic match would cause the House of Windsor. Libya's Colonel Gaddafi was the first to claim that the crash was the bloody result of anti-Arab activity, and the rumblings of popular suspicion and dissent have continued. Amongst the graffiti scrawled on the wall of the tunnel in Paris where the crash took place is the angry message, IT WAS NOT AN ACCIDENT BECAUSE THE 'IMPERIAL' FAMILY WILL NOT PERMIT TO HALFBREED CHILDREN HOWEVER THEYE (sic) ARE THE MOST BEAUTIFUL. In terms of race, religion and international relations, therefore, Diana in death and with regard to her position in relation to the Royal Family, is a significant figure. Perhaps for some she has the potential to become an Islamic martyr *avant la lettre*.

Even though most people do not go along with the conspiracy theories, many liberals, Muslims and multiculturalists have celebrated Diana's interest in Islamic and Asian cultures as a beacon of racial tolerance or even 'post-anti-racism'. Mica Nava, for example, writes, in an essay entitled 'Diana, Princess of Others: The Politics and Romance of "Race"', that what was

> *'most striking of all was her ability to speak and to recruit into her orbit those groups who considered themselves marginalised from the more orthodox political processes . . . The taken-for-grantedness of transracial, transcultural social encounters suggests a kind of post anti-racism, and marks a significant – if uneven – British cultural transformation that was reflected in the composition of her mourners after her death'.*[22]

Interestingly, this bears a remarkable similarity to the more right-wing libertarian position of Richard Littlejohn who saw in the ethnic and cultural diversity of Diana's mourners 'the kind of rainbow coalition which Ken Livingstone could only have dreamed about when he ran the old Greater London Council'. Littlejohn noted a form of natural or *laissez-faire* anti-racism that, for him, exposed the redundancy of 'political correctness' and other attempts to conceive actively anti-racist strategies; the presence of the multi-ethnic crowd at Diana Spencer's funeral provided a manifestation of racial harmony that can emerge organically without the manipulative hand of 'the left.'[23] Within this position, there is the lingering suggestion that in post-Diana Britain, we have transcended the need for pro-active political strategies, even that the product of anti-racism may be racism itself. Meanwhile, press photographs of people from different ethnic and cultural backgrounds gathered together and grieving for the Princess are seen as the progeny of the pictures of Diana meeting those from other cultures, expressing British multiculturalism at the level of the image.

## England's Rose

Paradoxically, then, the racial hatred expressed in various ways against the Fayeds bolsters the illusion of Diana as transracial, transcultural icon in her embrace of their difference. Rather than viewing Diana's death as the catalyst for a seismic shift in British culture, a moment symbolising the final stage of the development of racial and cultural tolerance, it is more convincing to view 'the Diana phenomenon' as a symptom of anxieties produced at the interstices of nation, race and culture in the global economy. These are highlighted both in the manner of her death and in the surprisingly global nature of the subsequent mourning.

Describing, in September 1997, increasing difficulties in dealing with a problem that crosses national frontiers, Lord Wakeham spoke of the menace of the paparazzi in terms analogous to the drugs trade, international terrorism and, by extension, disease.[24] His words revealed a metonymic relationship between the language of international crime prevention, the political rhetoric of immigration policy and the discourses of fear surrounding cultural and ethnic hybridity, with all their biological and viral resonances. Held to be at least partially to blame for the death of Diana, the internationally mobile, freelance paparazzo exposed the difficulties of policing national boundaries and of protecting precious national assets; Diana died in a foreign land, in foreign hands, as an effect of fleeing foreign photographers seeking to exploit the lucrative international trade in her image. Correspondingly, the grieving, too, was international , televised in the full sense of being arranged and performed for the global cameras. The composition of her 2.5 billion mourners worldwide and of those keen to view an event seen as historical before the fact no doubt epitomises the process of globalisation and power- fully demonstrates the easy traversability of national boundaries in a world increasingly dominated by the circulation of the image.

And where, in all this, was Diana, England's rose, recognised only after she had gone, and claimed as such, at least by Elton John and Bernie Taupin? Gone the way of the image, and even the language. Stuart Hall claims that this type of manifestation of global mass culture is a new field of visual representation itself.[25] While the West is undeniably the cultural powerhouse of the global economy, the process also being seen as an insidious form of Americanisation, the dynamic is not quite the same as earlier forms of imperialism. The image has no necessary national affiliation. Like the paparazzi who snapped the pictures of Diana, the image has no respect for the demands of national culture or boundaries. It has no need for transla- tion as it travels from one country to another, or *via* one satellite to a distant continent. The integrity of national culture as an ideal is irrelevant for these deterritorialising technologies and economies. For Stuart Hall, the path of the image has followed the trajectory of the English language which began in the glory days of the British

Empire. English, argues Hall, has undergone a series of transformations that have uprooted it from its origins and subverted its already rickety status as a national language, even as the first language of the United States of America:

> '[*the typical speakers of English*] *do not speak the Queen's English any longer. It speaks English as an international language which is quite a different thing. It speaks a variety of broken forms of English: English as it has been invaded, and as it has hegemonised a variety of other languages without being able to exclude them from it. It speaks Anglo-Japanese, Anglo-French, Anglo-German or Anglo-English indeed. It is a new form of international language, not quite the same old class-stratified, class-dominated, canonically secured form of standard or traditional highbrow English. That is what I mean by' centred in the West'. It is centred in the languages of the West, but not in the same way'.*[26]

It is a commonplace that the new technologies and globalised culture of supranational organisations like the multinational corporations that shape world markets, and superstates like the European Community that attempt to moderate them, have undermined the power and status of the traditional nation-state and national culture; it is even sometimes suggested that nations are clumsy and redundant obstacles to the efficient circulation of capital. As Jean-François Lyotard writes, the 'ideology of communicational transparency, . . . will begin to perceive the State as a factor of opacity and "noise"'.[27] In Britain, the clearest manifestation and acknowledgement of the cumulative effects of this process was the deregulation of the Stock Market and the subsequent 'Big Bang' in 1986, together with the chain of events that it produced, leading ultimately to 'Black Wednesday' and the destruction of the British Government's economic policy in 1992. Cain and Hopkins describe the function of the City of London now:

> '*As the imperial basis of its strength disappeared, the City survived by transforming itself into an 'offshore island' servicing the business created by the industrial and commercial growth of much more dynamic partners . . . The*

*City can now function successfully only by acting as an*
*intermediary for powers whose economies are far stronger*
*than Britain's*.[28]

Moreover, migration and geographical mobility has resulted in complex cultural identifications becoming the norm. Diana, then, insofar as she is presented as standing for tolerance and multiculturalism, associating with, befriending and representing a range of ethnic and cultural groups, would seem the perfect icon for the age. As an international celebrity, she does indeed seem to figure in a 'transracial, transcultural dimension', and her ubiquitous image seems infinitely appropriable, as the narrative of 'Muslim Diana' suggests, although it seems far-fetched to see this in terms of anti-racism.

Yet, simultaneously, Diana has been reclaimed as 'England's Rose'. The question this raises is whether the renaming of Diana is an affirmation of a newly rediscovered sense of authentic English identity, or just another appropriation, another product of ethnic marketing that takes advantage of the multi-identificatory power of Diana. After the trauma of her death, there were a variety of British attempts to re-narrativise the nation in relation to Diana and the groundswell of public emotion that spilled onto the streets in the weeks that followed it. There is no question that, since her death, Princess Diana has become a very potent figure in a set of national fantasies. In this way, I suggest, she functions in a way similar to the 'Thing' that, for the Lacanian political philosopher Slavoj Zizek, grounds a particular national fantasy in the 'real' – in this case in the traumatic reality of her death. The particular manifestation of the Thing illuminates, in turn, many of the anxieties caused by the receding power and influence of the nation-state in a global economy. Zizek argues that communities, including ethnic or national groupings, find their cohesion in a shared relationship towards an enjoyment that provides the affective substance present in a variety of social practices, rituals and collective myths. A certain enjoyment (an emotional, libidinal intensity) is invested in a certain phantasmatic Thing that comes to embody everything precious and intimate to the subject's sense of its own identity.

*'It is what is threatened when, for example, a white*
*Englishman is panicked because of the growing presence of*
*'aliens'. What he wants to defend at any price is not reduc-*
*ible to the so-called set of values that offer support to*

*national identity. National identification is by definition
sustained by a relationship toward the Nation* qua *Thing.
This Nation-Thing is determined by a series of contradictory properties. It appears to us as 'our ' Thing (perhaps we
could say* cosa nostra*), as something accessible only to 'us',
as something 'they', the others, cannot grasp; nonetheless it
is constantly menaced by them. It appears as what gives
plenitude and vivacity to our life, and yet the only way that
we can determine it is by resorting to different versions of
the same empty tautology. All we can ultimately say is that
the 'Thing' is 'itself', the' real thing', 'what it really is
about', etc. If we are asked how we can recognise the presence of this 'Thing', the only consistent answer is that the
'Thing' is present in that elusive entity called "our way of
life"'.* [29]

It is not simply that the Thing functions most powerfully when it is
threatened, it functions insofar as it is threatened; it emerges as an
effect of an indefinable threat or barrier to our enjoyment. Diana
functions, then, as a phantasmatic Thing in the English nationalist
narratives, retrospectively, as an effect of her death. It is the 'enjoyment 'with which the latter is invested – in *both* the image of
indestructible beauty noted by Scott Wilson in this volume, and
through the imagined *jouissance* of the crash[30]– that supports this
function of Diana as 'Nation-Thing'. In the intensity of the reactions to the details surrounding the crash, it is possible to identify a
narrative by which dead Diana became a placeholder for the national
Thing. She died in another country, having expressed her unhappiness at the difficulties she faced living in Britain, alongside a foreigner
unpopular in Britain, with a foreigner – later found to have exceeded
drink driving limits – at the wheel. It stirred many anxieties about
England's place in Europe that she died in a country whose economic
and foreign policy is central to many of the fears and prejudices held
by the British about European integration and the imagined
consequent loss of national sovereignty and identity. Worse still, the
car was fleeing foreign paparazzi. Naturally, the initial reaction of
the British media (particularly television news) was to blame them
for the death of Diana. Graphic and ugly stories about obstruction of
the emergency services, photographs taken of the fatally injured
Princess, even rumours of theft from and interference with the body

emerged. There was an almost immediate fascination and horror with the idea of foreign beings swarming like hungry insects over our beautiful Thing. At the same time, her death alongside Dodi was regarded as a horrific consummation of their affair, elevating him to the status of Romantic Hero and granting him privileged access to her *jouissance*, her beatific ecstasy in death. But why did she have to die in (or even at) the hands of these cruel or incompetent foreigners? Why didn't the Palace protect her? Why couldn't 'we' look after our own Princess? For some, like Lord Wakeham, this guilt and regret was inextricably tied to the difficulties posed by porous national boundaries and the decline of the authority of the nation. Diana's last movements re-enacted perfectly the precarious nature of our national Thing.

The events surrounding Diana's funeral and the retrospective narrative of her life, then, are an excellent illustration of Slavoj Zizek's thesis that national identity is sustained by its relationship to the fantasy of the nation *qua* Thing, the Thing which is exclusively 'ours' and beyond the comprehension of outsiders, yet is simultaneously threatened by them since they might 'steal' it. The apparently spontaneous reaction to her death, the thousands who drifted to Kensington Palace to lay flowers and poems and teddy bears but weren't sure why, the 'orderly queues' that formed to sign the books of condolence, the crowds that lined the streets of London on the day of her funeral,sombrely waiting for the cortège to pass, the wails of anguish as it did all serve to illustrate the operation of the national Thing, the 'disconnected fragments of the way our community organises its feasts, its rituals of mating, its initiation ceremonies and of course its funeral rites, in short, all the details by which a community organises its enjoyment'.[31] Using Zizek's formulation, this 'eruption of enjoyment into the social field', which is 'the privileged domain of nationalism' would be the reverse of the establishment of democracy, which involves the abstraction of the subject from its 'positive content', since only then can the subject of democracy become (necessarily) universalised.[32] The national specificity is the residue inherent in the process of democratisation, which constitutes the internal limit upon which it is predicated. Yet in attempting to explain the significance of the phenomenon of the mourning for Diana, meaning was located in ethnic and national interests; as the nation mourned for England's rose, it seemed that disparate and alienated individuals found themselves unsuspecting participants in an authentic organic community.

In relation to this, the idea of a truly 'multicultural' response to Diana's death looks less convincing, appearing more like a nostalgic colonial comfort in having members of immigrant communities 'follow our lead' in publicly mourning the Princess. Because she is England's rose she constitutes a disruption in the inaccessible enjoyment of the 'other '(as it is manifested in the ideological fantasy). Usefully, she also becomes a 'Tebbit test' for those of non-English or non-British ethnic backgrounds – and indeed for those unpatriotic liberals who failed to be moved by her death or participate in the ritual of public mourning. There are those who will willingly participate and embrace her and the host country as their own, and there are those whose presence undermines national cohesion. The question shifts from whether or not Britain is a safe, tolerant and plural environment for communities with different ethnic backgrounds, one in which cultural diversity might develop, to a question of which groups are stubbornly refusing to compromise or integrate. A tension is revealed within our 'enjoyment' of Diana and her passing: 'they' might have 'stolen' her in the guise of Dodi (or Islam, or America), yet there is also a nostalgic return to colonial relations in the images of the 'dazzling white goddess' continuing the British civilising mission through her humanitarian works – through 'bringing the benediction of birth control and beauty hints to an ambitious, agonised Third World'.[33]

## Ethnic Marketing

It has frequently been acknowledged that English, or British, identity and core values have come under increasing threat since the Second World War. Where Hitler failed to undermine the indomitable 'bulldog' spirit of British reaction to the Blitz, the more insidious culture of American capitalism (Hollywood, pop music, Coca-Cola) and European Federalism (decimal currency, agricultural policy, draining of sovereignty of Parliament) has succeeded in producing a transformation of the English or British way of life. One of the ironies of the Thatcher years was, of course, that her government's nationalist rhetoric masked a steady drain of British capital into foreign investments, the selling of key industries identified with Britain (Rover, Rolls Royce) into foreign hands, and afterwards, under the John Major premiership, the forging, through the Maastricht Treaty, of closer political and economic ties to the EU. Deliberately or not, Conservative rhetoric has tended to reify the nation as a smokescreen obscuring the nature of hypermodern capital. The confusion is evident in the following statement by Clive Aslet:

> *'It has become fashionable in some political circles to talk about Great Britain plc, as though it were a company, the implication being that everything can be expressed through the balance sheet. But if Britain really were a company, its board of directors would certainly have called in the marketing people to define its core values. They would then seek to test every activity and new initiative of the company by the degree to which it conformed to those core values. The core values of Britain are its identity. Much could be achieved if the government were to examine whether all the activities in which it has an interest express that Britishness'.* [34]

It ought to be obvious to Aslet that the only core values central to the success or survival of a company are economic ones, and that any cultural values dreamed up by marketing people are necessarily rigorously subordinate to such economic values; indeed, the whole point of marketing is to maximise the commercial potential of a particular product or company. Therefore, following the example of Manchester United plc, say, Great Britain plc would have to be sold to Rupert Murdoch if the price were favourable to the company's shareholders: that is the economic logic of the 'plc.' In fact, marketing people have indeed been called in to define and hone Britain's core values. These marketing people are called the New Labour Government and they have been busily testing every activity and new initiative by the degree to which it corresponds to core market values. In England, national identity is experienced as a commodity to be purchased, most commonly as a brand name or image: the Three Lions, Cool Britannia, National Parks, National Trust, English Heritage, and so on. Aslet's preposterous notion, his attempt to separate capitalism and state even as he subordinates the values of the latter to the former, is born out of the delusive fantasy of the nation as an autonomous actor with its own particular characteristics and agenda within a global hierarchy of nations, rather than as simply territory to be colonised by capital. Markets and brand identity are precisely the means through which nationalities, races, ethnic groups and regions are interpellated and isolated as 'niche markets.' The turn to nationalism, the ethnicisation of the nation, is part of this process because it seeks to hide and deny the victory of global capitalism over any alternative form of social organisation. As Zizek has argued, this can be seen most clearly in countries such as the former Yugoslavia, but versions can also be identified in Britain.

The characterisation of the Princess of Wales as 'England's rose' and the 'People's Princess' is, of course, part of this branding process, and it would no doubt be very instructive to know just how influential New Labour's marketing people were in the organisation and marketing of the funeral and its aftermath. Naturally, much of the English ethnic marketing was generated spontaneously and enthusiastically by the press in their effort to sell their papers. In the canon of photographs ceaselessly reproduced in the magazine supplements of the Sunday newspapers – Diana, Her Life In Pictures, Diana, A Life In Fashion/Style and so on – pictures appear of a 'shy chubby teenager' in riding gear, dressed for country pursuits. The invention of archaic Englishness, the fiction of origins, Albion, is invariably located in the rural. The young woman from the shires, the unspoilt girl from the unspoilt countryside. We were reminded how, when Charles married Diana, the strains of 'I Vow To Thee My Country' celebrated his public espousal to a little piece of England.

In death, it was to Englishness that Diana was returned as the international ambassador for England, the Queen of all our Hearts, driven through the Home Counties to be buried in the English countryside. This, significantly, was in contrast to the Windsors, whose Germanic origins were evoked with increasing regularity, and whose core values and protocol were seen to be increasingly archaic and irrelevant. If the mainstream media's line is to be believed, Diana has become the body upon which a New England can be built. Her significance for the nation and national identity is to be found in the gaps she created in traditional, aristocratic versions of Englishness, and in their relation to the 'modernisation' of that very 'newness' formulated by New Labour. Beatrix Campbell is one among many to associate the events of that September with the heady summer of Blairism, when journalists were falling over themselves to link Blair and Diana with a new emotionally literate politics that signified an emancipation of the British 'character' from the stultifying reserve associated with Britain's conservative past. Indeed, Blair publicly rebuked Anthony O'Hear on the steps of 10 Downing Street for suggesting that this sentimentalisation of Britain was fake.[35] Like Benedict Anderson's Tomb of the Unknown Soldier, the sudden death and absence of Diana seemed to become saturated with ghostly national imaginings.[36] 'Blair's Falklands' was won with the tag 'The People's Princess' (attributed to Alistair Campbell), and his 'authoritarian populism' (Stuart Hall)[37] was recast as the emergence of the People from the infantilising shadow of an ossified monarchy, articulating their regret at the years of Thatcherism and asserting their right to petition the monarch ('Show Us You Care' said _The Sun_ on its front page). The publicisation of Downing Street involvement in the funeral allowed the event and the figure of the crowd to become a manifestation of Blair's One Nation, but Blair's central role in the organisation of the civic rituals actually signified far more than offering the services of New Labour's formidable public relations machine to a remote and incompetent monarchy needing a spin. Blair co-opted the moment so successfully that, for a short while at least, it seemed he had actually become Diana. His suspension of party politics elevated him to her status above politics, and as he spoke, emotionally, for the nation, the people became incarnated in the one.[38]

The events in the week leading up to the funeral were reported as evidence of a new 'democratic' sense of popular participation among the people that was even imagined to be 'revolutionary' in the sense of a spontaneous uprising. I would argue, however, that it was not at all a democratic event, and that its very nature had serious and quite possibly worrying implications for any notion of multiculturalism in Britain. First, because the Blairite 'Tebbit Test' that demanded public avowals of emotion disenfranchised large sections of the population from New Labour's image of Britain; second, because this image of Britain is an effect of an economic system of marketing that has reference to democracy only to the degree to which it by-passes any appeal to rational faculties and instead appeals, manipulatively, towards the sorts of affections stirred by fiction. Further, these fictions depend, for their 'purchase' in the public imagination, on an unavowed racism that provides the 'spice' that adds flavour to a racy story (no pun intended). As I have begun to argue, Diana is most powerfully marketed as English when her proximity to the 'scumbag' Fayeds is emphasised: the Fayeds (and the concatenation of Islamic and Western Oriental references that they evoke) provide the 'threat' necessary to the full enjoyment of the national 'Thing'.

It is with the Fayeds that the issues of English national identity, Islam and Capital meet. An uncanny doubling unfolds in which British identity is sold to the British people in precisely the way that Mohamed Al-Fayed attempted to buy it. In the Mohamed Al-Fayed story, Diana is the 'ultimate trophy' in the pursuit and consumption of British identity (Harrods, Fulham, *Chariots of Fire*, the Estate of the Duke and Duchess of Windsor, and so on). While there may be distress at the thought of 'our' Princess falling into foreign hands, it is the tourist trade that is precisely used to justify the economic utility of the Royal Family; their value is precisely the effect of their consumption by foreign tourists. Fears about the consumption of Diana by the Fayeds disclose the anxiety about British commodification of its own core values, an anxiety that is highlighted when Muslims ('fundamentalist' or otherwise) are supposed to cherish *un*commodified values. There is the fear that Muslims 'really possess it', in the shape of 'traditional' family values, in their strict regulation of sexual morality and their belief in strong authority in contrast to the liberal decadence of the West. Behind the Western liberals criticisms of intolerance, fanaticism and misogyny there lurks a general fear that this account may be true. Evidence for this can be found in the general appeal to family responsibility, conservative morality, clean living, and so on, across the contracting spectrum of British political discourse. Therefore, Diana's turning to a Muslim after a failed marriage and a lifetime of 'family disaster' might have been 'really getting It' - the full phallic power of patriarchal law. Hence, correlatively, the enjoyment and excitement at stories of Dodi's sexual potency: his attraction to other white women and the (subsequently disproved) claim that he had fathered a 'love child'.

## The End(s) of Racism

Slavoj Zizek's Lacanian mentor Jacques-Alain Miller figures the relationship of the West to its Other in the following way:

*'In racism, it is precisely a question of the relation to an
Other as such, conceived in its difference. And it does not
seem to me that any of the generous and universal discourses
on the theme of 'we are all fellow beings' have had any
effectiveness concerning this question. Why? Because racism
calls into play a hatred which goes precisely towards what
grounds the Other's alterity, in other words its* jouissance.
*If no decision, no will, no amount of reasoning is sufficient
to wipe out racism, it is indeed because it is founded on the
point of extimacy of the Other . . . Racism is founded on
what one imagines about the Other's* jouissance . . . *We
may well think that racism exists because our Islamic
neighbour is too noisy when he has parties . . . Racist stories
are always about the way in which the Other obtains a*
'plus de jouir': *either he does not work or he does not work
enough, or he is useless or a little too useful, but whatever
the case may be, he is always endowed with a part of*
jouissance *he does not deserve'.*[39]

Like Zizek, Miller locates racism in extimacy (intimate exteriority)
and argues that it manifests itself in the ascription to the other of
excess *jouissance* – too much 'enjoyment' (*plus de jouir* or surplus
enjoyment). This, of course, is independent of the behaviour of the
Other who might be regarded as either decadent, lazy and voracious,
or as too efficient. The *plus du jouir* is not the cause but the internal
support of racialised difference. Yet for hypermodern capital, this
racist mistrust is entirely inseparable from a desiring relationship
toward the Other. Quite obviously, it is 'enjoyment' that we want to
buy when we exchange our hard-earned cash for some desirable
goods. It is through consumption that we imagine we gain our share
of the enjoyment located in the Other (the system of commodity
capitalism) whose point of alterity is precisely located in the *plus de
jouir* of the racialised other. In other words, difference is exoticised
and becomes the combustion engine of consumption. The Other
comes to stand for the exotic, the erotic, the dangerous and the
authentic; in the face of anxieties about bland and homogenising
Western consumer culture, effacing difference beneath the golden
arches of McDonalds or the colonising power of Coca Cola, 'they'
either violently and terroristically resist the imperialism of the West
or fall victim to it, in which case their 'sacrifice' or 'rape' lends an

authentic, sovereign value to that which was lost. Capital locates consumer desire in the Other that is both the subject and object of its ethnic marketing. The Other becomes the spice to pep up dreary Americanised lives in the West, and it makes little difference whether this other can be located in the rainforests of Brazil or on Brick Lane, East London. This, of course, betrays the complicity of liberal multiculturalism, and its concern for the preservation of authenticity, with capital, and calls into question its anti-racist integrity. Stuart Hall describes how the shape of hypermodern capital enables the consumption of the Other, elevating it to the level of an imperative:

> '*Certain forms of advertising are still grounded on the exclusive, powerful, dominant, highly masculinist, old Fordist imagery, of a very exclusive set of identities. But side by side with them are the new exotica. To be at the leading edge of modern capitalism is to eat fifteen different cuisines in any one week, not to eat one. It is no longer important to have boiled beef and carrots and Yorkshire pudding every Sunday. Who needs that? Because if you are just jetting in from Tokyo, via Harare, you come in loaded, not with how 'everything is the same' but how wonderful it is, that 'everything is different'. In one round trip around the world, in one weekend, you can see every wonder of the ancient world. You take it in as you go by, all in one, living with difference, wondering at pluralism, this concentrated, corporate, over-corporate, over-integrated, over-concentrated, and condensed form of economic power which lives culturally through difference and which is constantly teasing itself with the pleasures of the transgressive Other'.*[40]

Stuart Hall here demonstrates how the commodification and deterritorialisation of hypermodern capital depends upon the generalisation of the restricted economy, how homogenisation ('everything is the same') depends upon the consumption of heterogeneity ('everything is different'). The relationship to the transgressive Other is crucial in this regard. Capital's own transgressive progress depends upon constructing a transgressive Other to fuel consumer desire, either as a point of exotic difference or as a point of prohibition, an imagined barrier, a veil, to that desire. These days ,difference, alterity, even the sacred itself is located in transgression. This, in itself, connotes a shift in the nature of the sacred. While the banality of Stuart Hall's association of this transgressive Other with eclectic cuisine may fail to convince some, a better example might be the series of Benetton adverts that have been running since the Eighties and have used hitherto taboo images (bloody, newly born baby, the death-bed AIDS scene, the black child with Devil's horns and so on) in order to sell their knitwear. Similarly, during the controversy surrounding the publication of *The Satanic Verses*, the images of the Muslim book-burners in Bradford came to stand for the crisis and the incommensurability of the two value systems, the Western and the Islamic. For horrified Western liberals, this scene evoked similar immolations in Nazi Germany and signified the dangers of a totalising value system, yet it was precisely around the outrage the image provoked that their position was organised. Significantly, the Islamic community in Bradford, no doubt learning fast the economic law of the image, had shot the book burning sequence themselves precisely in order to sell the film to TV companies, reaping thousands in royalties for their campaign. Gilles Kepel describes them, perhaps a little condescendingly, as the children of Marshall MacLuhan and compares the nature of, and the reaction to, the short film with the grainy amateur pictures of the attack in Los Angeles on Rodney King.[41]

Images of racial equality or harmony signify differently. Take as an example the 'One to One' mobile 'phone advertisement featuring Ian Wright, the former Arsenal and England striker with an explosive scoring and disciplinary record. Wright tells us that if space, time and mortality were not factors, he would choose to have his 'one to one' with Martin Luther King. Making implicit reference to his own outbursts on the football pitch, some of which have undoubtedly been in response to racist provocation, Wright confesses that he would ask the human rights activist how to turn the other cheek in such situations. This, while a laudable sentiment within the context of a Western Judeo-Christian value system apparently endorsed by King, positions Wright as a figure who would like to operate within the rules of the footballing authorities rather than remain a problematic figure for them. This can be seen, too, in the Nike adverts also featuring Ian Wright, and those featuring Eric Cantona that operate on a transgressive image which appropriates anti-racism in order to sell the sportswear of a corporation with alleged exploitative worker conditions in Vietnam.[42] The logic is essentially the same with US record companies deploying Black American Gansta rap artists and their associations with violent gang warfare, crime, drugs, misogyny and certain versions of Black power, the major market for which is in the white suburbs. The key element is the transgressive quality of the image that is sold. I would suggest that the same logic applies even to the marketing of 'Islamic Fundamentalism' both in everyday news stories, for home consumption, and as the imaginary limit of global capitalism: the barrier that provides the very point of resistance and desirability (and the alibi) for the political facilitation of US capital in Islamic parts of the world. In this way the spectre of Islamic Fundamentalism operates just as Communism did during the Cold War.

In this context, the Fayeds' function is a doubled and reversible way. Mohamed Al-Fayed too readily, too abjectly sought, bought yet failed ultimately to acquire the Britishness he coveted; it crumbled in his hands. Perhaps the loathing of this 'Arab merchant' by certain parts of the press has much to do with an unconscious recognition of the tawdry, commodified nature of British identity itself, of a Britain seeking endlessly to 'market itself', a Britain that has not ceased to sell itself and its Empire with an increasing sense of desperation throughout the post-War Cold War period. Indeed, A.N. Wilson's review of the biography of Al-Fayed concludes bitterly with a list of Establishment figures who sold themselves, in one way or another, to his 'Feikery', a list that culminates, of course, with the Princess of Wales herself.[43]

## References

1   Leslie White, *Sunday Times* 7 September 1997, see http:// www. Sunday-times.co.uk/news/pages/sti/97/09/stirevopno 10.2.html?999
2   Salman Rushdie, *The New Yorker* 15 September 1997, p.69
3   See 'Dodi, a Playboy in the Fast Lane' *The Observer* 7 September 1997, pp. 18–19.
4   Camille Paglia, *Salon Magazine* cited in *The Guardian* 4 September 1997, p.17.
5   Tom Bower, *Fayed: The Unauthorised Biography*, London: MacMillan, 1998.
6   Henry Porter, *The Guardian*, Saturday Review, 24 October 1998, p.1
7   A.N. Wilson, *The Guardian*, Saturday Review, 24 October 1998 p.8
8   Julie Burchill, *The Guardian*, 2 September 1997, p. 5.
9   A.N. Wilson, *The Guardian*, 24 October 1998, p. 8
10  From Ian Hislop (ed.) *The Best of Private Eye 1987-89*: 'The Satanic Verses' by Salmonella Bordes. London, Private Eye Productions/ Andre Deutsch, 1989. p. 8
11  Sigmund Freud, *Jokes and Their Relation to the Unconscious*, London, Penguin 1991. p. 232

12  It is interesting to note that many contemporary manifestations of Englishness and English nationalism, particularly those that are a product of 'new lad' culture, turn upon the same disavowal of serious intent.

13  Marcia Pointon, 'A Latter-Day Siegfried: Ian Botham at the National Portrait Gallery, 1986'. *New Formations*, Post-Colonial insecurities, 21 (Winter 1993) pp. 131-145, p. 142.

14  *The Guardian*'s Mike Selvey, 27 August 1992, in Chris Searle, 'Cricket and the Mirror of Racism', *Race and Class* 34. 3 (1993) pp.45-54, p.45.

15  The succession to the throne is still, of course, governed by the Act of Settlement which states that 'whosoever shall hereafter come to the possession of this Crown shall join in communion with the Church of England as by law established' (Act of Settlement, 1701).

16  http//www.albany.edu/-ha4934/imran.khan

17  *Daily Mail* 1 September 1997, p.17

18  See also Susannah Frankel in *The Guardian*, who wrote how Diana was 'attributed with anticipating a return to ethnic style'. 2 September 1997, p.2.

19  *Daily Mirror*, 1 September, 1997, p. 38

20  *The Observer* 7 October 1997, p.5

21  Theodore Zeldin, 'Smiles Herald a New Age: The End of Cynism' *The Observer* Commemorative Edition, 7 September 1997, p. 22.

22  Mica Nava in *Planet Diana: Cultural Studies and Global Mourning*, ed. Re: Public Research Centre in Intercommunal Studies, University of Western Sydney, 1998.

23  Richard Littlejohn, *The Daily Mail*, 4 September 1997, p. 11.

24  Lord Wakeham, *The Guardian* 2 September 1997, p.1

25  Stuart Hall, 'The Local and the Global: Globalisation and Ethnicity' in Anthony D. King (ed) *Culture, Globalisation and the World System*, London, Macmillan 1991. pp. 19-39, p.31

26  Hall, 'The Local and the Global' p. 28.

27  Jean-François Lyotard, *The Postmodern Condition*, Manchester, Manchester University Press, 1979 p. 5.

28  P.J. Cain and A.G. Hopkins, *British Imperialism: Crisis and Deconstruction 1914-1990*. Harrow, Longman, 1993, pp. 293-6.

29  Slavoj Zizek, *Tarrying with the Negative*, Durham, Duke University Press, 1993, p. 201. For Zizek on enjoyment see also *For They Know Not What They Do: Enjoyment as a Political Factor*, London, Verso, 1991 and *The Metastases of Enjoyment*, London, Verso, 1996, among others.

30  See Scott Wilson, above.

31  Zizek, *Tarrying*, p. 202.

32  Ibid.

33  Burchill, *The Observer*, 7 September 1997, p. 20.

34  Clive Aslet, *Anyone for England: A Search for British Identity*, London: Little, Brown and Co., 1997, p. 246.

35  See Anthony O'Hear, 'Diana, Queen of Hearts' in Digby Anderson

and Peter Muller (eds.) *Faking It: The Sentimentalisation of Modern Society*, London: Social Affairs Unit, 1998.

36  Beatrix Campbell, *Diana, Princess of Wales: How Sexual Politics Shook the Monarchy*, London: The Women's Press, 1998.

37  Stuart Hall: 'The Local and the Global;' p. 31

38  It should be noted that Blair has always sought to use the mythical body of the people in two characteristic ways. 1. He tries to be a reflection of the people. 2. He uses the people as a stick to beat the Left in his own party; i.e.he's got a bigger democratic mandate than they can offer. This happened before the election on the basis that he had a 'feel' for what the nation wanted. Mention also that this event allowed Blair to be 'genuine' and 'spontaneous', thus undermining the popular view that he was too reliant upon spin and soundbites.

39  Jacques Alain Miller, 'Extimité', *Prose Studies*, 11 (1988) pp.125-6.

40  Stuart Hall , 'The Local and the Global' p. 31

41  G. Kepel, *Allah in the West: Islamic Movements in America and Europe*, tr. Susan Milner, Cambridge, Polity, 1997. p. 81

42  See Verena Dobnik, 'Nike Told of Abuses in Vietnam' in Julie Rivkin and Michael Ryan (eds), *Literary Theory: An Anthology*, Oxford, Blackwell, 1998, pp. 328–323.

43  A.N. Wilson, *The Guardian* 24 October 1998. p.8

# 5. Diana's Self and the Quest Within

## Paul Heelas

*' I have learned much over the last years. From now on I am going to own myself and be true to myself. I no longer want to live someone else's idea of what and who I should be. I am going to be me'.* [1]

Diana, Princess of Wales, 1993.

Diana drew upon a range of experts to try to improve the quality of her life. In alphabetical order, and mentioning only some of those introduced by Andrew Morton in his *Diana, Her New Life*[2], there is the 'adviser', 'astrologer', 'business motivator guru', 'clairvoyant', 'confidant', 'counsellor', 'exercise trainer', 'fitness teacher', 'gym trainer', 'homeopathic doctor', 'hypnotherapist', 'lifestyle manager', 'masseur', 'mystic', 'New Age therapist', 'osteopath', 'psychotherapist', 'sleep therapist', 'soothsayer', 'spiritual adviser', 'tarot-card reader', 'therapist', and 'voice coach'. Some of the experts, such as psychotherapist Susie Orbach, focused on dealing with the past; others, such as astrologer Debbie Frank, concentrated on what was in store in the future; and yet others, including osteopath Michael Skipwith and masseur Stephen Twigg, were on hand to deal with immediate practicalities, such as 'feeling right' for an important event. Coverage by the experts, it would appear, was pretty comprehensive: not only with regard to the past, present and future, but also with regard to the realms of the body, the psychological and the mystical.

Dwelling on what expertise has to offer with regard to (broadly conceived) spirituality or religiosity, a noticeable omission concerns any reference to the vicar (or priest). Taking other evidence into account, it is safe to say that Diana showed little enthusiasm for traditional religion.

In contrast, however, she was very much concerned with what the traditionalist would take to be unorthodox, if not false. Her concerns, that is to say, were with what lies beyond church and chapel: the astrologer, tarot-card reader; the New Age therapist.

One task, in what follows, is to explore the beliefs, values and assumptions which served to inform Diana's self-understanding, especial attention being paid to her search 'within': her quest to find, 'own' and express her-self; her search for 'inner' spirituality. Another is to argue that, but for her death, Diana's growing concern with 'New Age' teaching and practices means that it seems highly likely that she would have gone on to become an emblematic figure of the New Age Movement, serving as an exemplar of that form of spirituality which involves the sacralisation of the self. The fact of her death, however, prompts another argument, to do with how the death of her 'heart' brought to 'life' all those of the population who would never dream of describing themselves as spiritual beings, but who nevertheless have faith in what their personal lives have to offer. And finally, by way of introduction, attention is also paid to more general considerations: Diana as exemplifying – in key regards – why people seek out New Age provisions; Diana as an excellent illustration of those who engage in 'spiritual shopping' to resource their lives; and Diana as being far from exceptional when it compared with the – broadly conceived – spirituality found among cultural elites.

## The New Age Movement

Before looking at Diana's beliefs in any detail, I first sketch what I mean by the term 'New Age Movement'. This sketch should help us avoid those confusions which arise from the fact that the term has been used in a variety of ways. Furthermore, and more importantly, the sketch provides a framework for looking more closely at the nature of Diana's activities beyond church and chapel.

There are three fundamental assumptions. The first is that peoples' lives are not working. We have all been infected by the discontents of the modern world. We have all been socialised into erroneous, mechanistic, artificial, superficial forms of life. Some of us might suffer from the sense of not having achieved enough; others of us might feel jaded by success. Whatever the specifics, the New Age claim is that life in the everyday world is flawed; is far from perfect.

The second assumption is that life need not be like this. For beyond the self which has been constructed by the institutions and discourses of the modern world, lies a realm of being which is perfect in and of itself. That is to say, beyond the 'lower self' or 'ego' lies the realm of the 'Higher Self', 'inner spirituality', the 'Goddess within', the 'Life Force', the 'Light'. This is what we all are by nature, by essence. This is the realm of true or authentic love, vitality, energy, wisdom, peace, truth, responsibility, harmony, tranquillity, ('magical') power, health: the ultimates of what 'life' has to offer.

As for the third assumption, those involved with the New Age not surprisingly suppose that it is possible to move from life solely in the hands of the 'ego' to life informed by what lies embedded within. Few might think that it is possible to become permanently 'enlightened', it being widely held that the 'ego' has very considerable 'survival' power. But all think that it is possible to engage in practices (rituals, meditations, workshops, retreats, etc.) to experience the inner realm – and thereby 'transform' the quality of life.

Although these three assumptions are to be found in teaching after teaching, ritual after ritual, indeed, book after book, it is essential to note that there are also important variations on the theme of the New Age quest within. Some practitioners (to varying degrees) are world-rejecting, believing that the best way to handle ego-attachments is to steer well clear of capitalistic modernity; others (also to varying degrees) are world-affirming, believing that it is possible to deploy inner spirituality in order to become more successful within the mainstream. Another significant variation concerns where New Agers turn for inspiration and activities, some drawing on eastern mystical traditions, others the 'pagan', yet others on western therapies. Then there are differences to do with focus of interest: the body and health; emotions and psychological well-being; nature and holistic experiences; the will to power and advancement.

To complete this brief sketch, and very much with an eye on the analysis to follow, it remains to emphasise one crucial point. It concerns experience of the Self as the locus of authority. The matter can be approached by considering Michael Perry's summary of a talk delivered by Sir George Trevelyan. Perry reported that Trevelyan

> *'spoke a great deal of theology, and obviously was drawing on a great bank of doctrine, but he was insistent that dogma was one of the curses of religion. He resolved the paradox,*

*in true New Age fashion, by saying, in effect "This is what
things look like to me. If it doesn't seem like that to you,
you don't have to accept what I say.* Only accept what
rings true to your own Inner Self."[3]

With God or the Goddess dwelling at the core of the person, it is
only to be expected that experience of that which lies within provides
the ultimate authority or source of truth. Putative sources of authority
emanating from beyond the Higher Self, such as those provided by
religious traditions or dogmas, have to be tested by way of the
touchstone of one's own 'inner' experience. For religious traditions
(etc.) could well be unreliable, contaminated by all those 'egos' which
have helped sustain tradition through history. Tradition, indeed any
'external' source of authority, is not to be trusted *per se*. And this
assessment is enhanced by the strong momentum, within New Age
circles, to reject anything which threatens the freedom, control,
power, creativity, responsibility bound up with the life of the Higher
Self.

In sum, the thrust of the New Age is in favour of
detraditionalisation, to the point - in some quarters - where
spirituality is envisaged in post-traditional fashion. The Self is in
control. To be dictated to, to be dependent on the beliefs and values
of others, is to lose touch with what alone really counts: personal,
spiritually-informed experience.[4]

## Astrology, Soothsaying, Clairvoyance, and a Witchdoctor

Turning to the nature of Diana's beliefs and practices beyond church
and chapel, one of the most arresting things likely to strike the reader,
of, say, Morton' s *Diana, Her New Life* and *Diana, Her True Story -
In Her Own Words*, Julie Burchill's *Diana*, or Beatrix Campbell's
*Diana, Princess of Wales*, is the importance she attached to what many
would consider to be paranormal or supernatural powers, in
particular those to do with predicting the future.[5] For it would appear
- in the words of Campbell - that here was a 'superstitious woman
who seemed to spend as much money on astrologers and psychics as
ordinary mortals might actually earn'.[6]

To provide several illustrations of the role played by experts of
the paranormal, Morton writes, 'With one of her soothsayers, she

will plot Camilla's astrological chart – like Diana she is Cancerian – and then she mulls over the runes'; 'A consultation with her soothsayer greatly unsettled her. She predicted that two weeks after the full moon, which was due to fall on 30 October [1993], Prince Charles would face a major upset in his life'; 'The timing [of her announcement that she was withdrawing from public life] owed as much to her astrologer as it did to the royal calendar. The astrologer had indicated that early December would be a propitious time for the Princess of make decisive changes in her life'; and, 'France appears time and again in her private astrological prophecies both as a future home and the birthplace of the new man in her life'.[7]

As will be apparent, Diana's astrologers and soothsayers (in particular) often provided her with very concrete, specific predictions. In connection with another example, this leads Morton to conclude:

> 'Her belief, at times all consuming, in the predictions of her astrologer, shows how little value she placed on her own instincts and judgment. The astrologer had forecast, for example, that the end of 1993 would bring a 'golden opportunity' for the Princess in the form of a prestigious job, and while Diana waited for this chance to fall into her lap, the more sceptical of her friends suggested that people make their own luck in life'.[8]

It is as though the future is laid out in advance, what Morton sees as Diana's lack of self-esteem (he also refers to her 'insecurity and self-denigration') being associated with her *dependency* on what the experts state is going to happen. Indeed, this dependency is not limited to the future. For it is also seen in the fact, as Morton puts it, that 'The Princess often explains the actions of her friends by reference to characteristics typical of their particular signs of the zodiac'. In addition, dependency is also in evidence in her deployment of clairvoyants, Morton writing:

> 'Since then [the death of Scotland Yard bodyguard Inspector Barry Mannakee in 1987] she has used a clairvoyant to try and contact Mannakee and dead family relatives, particularly her uncle, Lord Fermoy, who committed suicide, and her much-loved grandmother Cynthia

*Spencer. She had told friends that Mannakee, "meant an
awful lot to me. He was my father figure and looked after
me."*[9]

It is absolutely clear that the beliefs and activities under consideration played an important role in Diana's life. Dating from early adult-
hood, if not before, they were still very much in evidence at the time
of her death: in March 1997 - and on the advice of Nelson Mandela -
she contacted South African 'witchdoctor' Credo Mutwa; in the
months before she died she was trying to arrange a meeting in London
with people interested in spiritualism; and very shortly before her
death, she flew with Dodi, in a Harrods helicopter, to consult with
clairvoyant Rita Rogers in Chesterfield.[10]

But does all this provide evidence that Diana was involved in
New Age spirituality? I think not. The reason is clear-cut. Given the
characterisation of the New Age Movement provided earlier, where
attention was directed to the immense authority and value attributed
to experiential Self-spirituality, there is too much dependency; too
much reliance on external agencies - from the stars to the dead; too
much emphasis on an laid-down order of things beyond one's control
and therefore beyond one's responsibility.[11]

## Encouraging New Age Spirituality

We have to look elsewhere to support our thesis that Diana was set
fair to becoming a key player within New Age circles. In order to
argue that over the years Diana became increasingly interested in
what the New Age has to offer, let us begin with her honeymoon. In
her 'own words',

> *'Charles used to want to go for long walks around Balmoral
> the whole time we were on our honeymoon. His idea of
> enjoyment would be to sit on top of the highest hill at
> Balmoral. It is beautiful up there. I completely understand;
> he would read Laurens van der Post or Jung to me, and
> bear in mind I hadn't a clue about psychic powers or
> anything, but I knew there was something in me that hadn't
> awakened yet and I didn't think this was going to help!'*[12]

Jung and van der Post; the former strongly influencing the latter;
both advocates of what we are here calling New Age spirituality; and

neither being of much - if any - significance for Diana. Yet by the end of her life she was making contact with people who, in many regards, are latter-day 'van der Postians'.

Unfortunately, although perhaps not surprisingly, I have not been able to find any detailed accounts of what Diana's 'gurus' actually taught her. However, by looking at what these contacts have written about their own teachings, we can reasonably infer what they would have been saying to Diana - and (presumably) what she would have been finding of value.

Consider, briefly, Anthony Robbins, describing himself at the beginning of his *Unlimited Power. The New Science of Personal Achievement* as 'the founder and president of Robbins Research Institute, an international network of professionals dedicated to the advancement of human potential in bioscience, accelerated learning, neurolinguistics, and child development.'[13] Meeting Diana for the first time in 1995 (it appears), Robbins emphasises the importance of 'pattern interrupt' (to weaken the limiting effects of the ego); writes that 'You have the resources to take absolute charge of your life'; states that 'To say that there is no source of intelligence that we may call God is like saying *Webster's Dictionary* is the result of an explosion in a print factory and everything came together perfectly and in balance'; and affirms: 'You can create the powerful beliefs and states that will produce miracles for you and the people you care about. But it will happen only if you make it happen'.[14]

Or consider, equally briefly, the highly influential New Age teacher, Deepak Chopra. According to Anna Pasternak, 'The smartest spiritual spa in the United States, Chopra's centre [the Chopra Center for Well Being] is the epitome of 1990s chic. His apostles include Demi Moore, Michael Jackson, Elizabeth Taylor, Donna Karan, Hillary Clinton and the late Diana, Princess of Wales'. Pasternak then goes on to quote Chopra on the capacities of what lies within:

> 'To make the right choices in life, you have to get in touch with your soul. To do this, you need to experience solitude, which most people are afraid of, because in the silence you hear the truth and know the solutions. I realised early on that we don't have to be victims of our situations. With the right attitude, we can generate the experiences we want in our lives'.

And then, with specific reference to Diana, Pasternak asks, 'if, on a subconscious level, we draw every experience to us, why did Diana, Princess of Wales, with whom Chopra had lunch shortly before her death, want to die? The guru then says:

> *'From a Jungian and spiritual insight, I would say Yes.*
> *She had the sinner and the saint in her, running parallel,*
> *and subconsciously she orchestrated the whole thing because*
> *she wanted to be outrageous.*[15]

Thinking back to her honeymoon, despite her marked lack of response to Jung and van der Post, Diana nevertheless claims that she 'knew there was something in me that hadn't awakened yet'. By the end of her life, however, she was being attracted by leading New Age figures who have a great deal to say about the nature and capacities of this 'something'. Indeed, through Chopra (for example) Diana was hearing Jung - but now (one has to assume) as a great, wise teacher.

Finally, it should be noted that Diana's encounter with New Age spirituality was by no means limited to Robbins and Chopra. Although there is very little hard evidence, it is difficult to believe that Diana - by the time of her death - was not immersed in (aspects of) New Age spirituality by many of the experts to whom she turned. Therapists attending to her body, health, vitality and beauty are of particular significance in this regard. For whether it be deep-tissue massage, aromatherapy, acupuncture, cranial massage, osteopathy, the Hay diet or *tai-chi*, Diana would have encountered (typically eastern) themes and assumptions. *Tai-chi* provides an excellent illustration, Diana stating that when people ask 'what do you know about *tai-chi*?', she replies 'An energy flow', continuing, 'and they look at me and they say: "She's the girl who's supposed to like shopping and clothes the whole time. She's not supposed to know about *spiritual* things"'.[16]

In addition, it is also safe to assume that Diana encountered beliefs and assumptions (if not experiences) of 'inner spirituality' through her contacts with close 'confidants' like Oliver Hoare (expert on Islamic Sufi mysticism), her reading of books on the power of positive thinking and healing, and, for that matter, through at least some of her astrologers (astrologer Felix Lyle, for example, stating 'The potential is there. She is a flower waiting to bud').[17]

Overall, by the end of here life it is clear that Diana was by no means uninformed about New Age teachings, practices - and, one ventures, experiences. At the same time, and to introduce a point to which we will return, there would appear to be no (published) evidence of Diana speaking as a 'fully-fledged' New Ager. Shirley MacLaine might say 'I am God. I am God. I am God'; at least in public, Diana was much more circumspect, generally deploying - as we shall see, more ' expressivistic' or 'humanistic' language.[18]

## Diana's 'heart'

Having discussed two 'strands' of Diana's self-understanding - provided by experts of the paranormal and those directly concerned with inner spirituality - it remains to discuss Diana's 'heart', that is, Diana the 'expressivist'. As well as enabling us to arrive at a more comprehensive picture of her understanding of *herself*, this discussion also serves as a vital step in the argument that by the time of her death Diana was poised to become a 'fully-fledged' adherent of New Age spirituality.

First, though, what does it mean to speak of 'expressivism', and what is the evidence that Diana was - perhaps predominantly - 'expressivist'? An excellent introduction to this mode of selfhood is provided by Edward Shils, in a passage which deserves to be cited at some length:

> *'There is a belief, corresponding to a feeling, that within each human being there is an individuality, lying in potentiality, which seeks an occasion for realisation but is held in the toils of the rules, beliefs, and roles which society imposes. In a more popular, or vulgar, recent form, the concern to 'establish one's identity', 'to discover oneself', or to 'find out who one really is' has come to be regarded as a first obligation of the individual. Some writers on undergraduate education in the United States say that a college is a place where young people can 'find out who they really are'. They suggest that the real state of the self is very different from the acquired baggage which institutions like families, schools, and universities impose. To be 'true to oneself', means, they imply, discovering what is contained in the uncontaminated self, the self which has been freed from*

> *the encumbrance of accumulated knowledge, norms, and*
> *ideals handed down by previous generations.*[19]

The expressive mode, it will immediately be seen, follows the same basic logic as New Age spirituality: there is an outer realm, imposed by the institutional order and resulting in false consciousness; there is an inner realm which provides true identity and which therefore must be sought out. Furthermore, it can be added, expressivists generally share much the same values or valued states of being with their New Age companions: self-fulfillment, growth, authenticity, honesty, generosity and compassion, for example. Finally, it needs to be emphasised that although the expressive mode, as summarised by Shils, has much in common with New Age teaching, there is one crucial difference: the self of the former is envisaged in psychological-cum-humanistic fashion; the self of the latter is envisaged as being explicitly spiritual.

What, then, is the evidence that Diana was expressivistic? There is in fact evidence galore - to the extent that one is strongly inclined to conclude that this was the dominant discourse of her 'own' life. Beginning with how she talked about what lies within, there is no better place to commence than the *Panorama* interview of November, 1995. In one of the most memorable statements, Diana says, 'I would like to be Queen in people's hearts, but I don't think many [Establishment] people would want me to be Queen. I do things differently, because I don't follow the rule book, because I lead from the heart, not the head'.[20] The basic idea here - that truth is somehow an expression of what lies within - was affirmed time and time again by Diana during her lifetime. During the *Panorama* interview itself, for example, there is the cry, 'Oh, a woman's instinct is a very good one'. Or one might think of statements cited by Morton, including: '*A voice said to me inside*: "You won't be Queen but you'll have a tough role"'; 'I will make mistakes but that will not stop me doing what *I feel is right*'; and 'Nobody expected me to turn up [to Camilla's sister's 40th birthday party] but again a *voice inside me* said: "Go for the hell of it"'.[21]

On the one hand, highly positive evaluations of the 'heart', 'feelings', 'instincts' (and 'intuitions'), the 'myself' and 'me' of the statement with which this chapter commenced. Conversely, and in accord with the logic of expressivism, she also held highly negative evaluations of established, routinised orders; what she felt to be imposed, restrictive and artificial. According to Morton, for example, 'she believes that she is still the "PoW" - prisoner of Wales - her life constrained by the royal system, the detritus of a failed marriage and an eager and voracious mass media'.[22] Duties to perform - especially with regard to the royal *system*; roles which have to be played - for example whilst on royal tours; there was much which did not accord with her expressive spirit.

As for the values associated with her expressivism, Morton writes of her 'refreshing openness and willingness to build bridges'; her ability to 'forgive'; her 'generous heart'; her 'spontaneity'. He also writes of her solution to what she took to be pitfalls caused by male 'pride', namely 'provid[ing] a softer, feminine approach, using her sensitivity and intuition to help unblock choked lines of discussion'. As for the responses of others, Morton writes of those charity workers, homeless people, AIDS sufferers, the sick, and battered women who 'talk of the Princess's generous spirit her genuine empathy with society's victims'; of all those who affirm, 'She really seemed to understand me. It came from the heart'. And now, as Morton reports the words of Diana herself 'The more honest you are, the better you feel'; and, 'if we can help give them [women dependent on tranquillisers and other drugs] their right to fulfil their own potential, maybe fewer women would find themselves living a life that is bleak beyond belief'.[23] Or one can think of what Diana had to say during the *Panorama* interview:

> '*I love being with people*'; .. '*my goodness, I've had to grow*'; '*I want them [my children] to have an understanding of people's emotions, people's distress, and people's hopes and dreams*'; and, '*I found myself being more and more involved with people who were rejected by society.... and I found an affinity there. And I respected very much the honesty I found on that level with people I met, because in hospices, for instance, when people are dying they're much more open and more vulnerable, and much more read than other people*'.[24]

Diana's humanistic, expressive values (compassion, generosity, empathy, of 'belonging one to another' as she said during a speech about the Commonwealth) were intimately bound up with expressive values of a somewhat more inner, psychological orientation (growth, fulfilling potential, exploring buried, negative emotions to find release, nurturing positive emotions, understanding what lies at the heart of people beyond their public 'acts').[25] Furthermore, many of the activities to which Diana turned were very much to do with the expressive. Psychotherapy or the gym, for example, provided Diana the opportunity to 'be' herself, to grow, to express her nature, the 'temple' that was her body. And at the same time, such activities served to address negative experiences and emotions: in the case of colonic irrigation, for example, Diana feeling that the irrigations 'take all the aggro out of me'.[26]

In sum, though it would be utterly mistaken for us to conclude that Diana was simply a (humanistic/ psychologistic) expressivist (her dealings with the Royal Family, for example, clearly show that she was not in the least immune to being deceitful), it is surely impossible to deny the fact that discourses of the heart played a central role in her life.

## Diana's 'conversion career'[27]

Taking stock, we have been exploring three – distinctive, albeit sometimes interplaying – 'strands' or 'dimensions' of Diana's self-understanding. We began with consideration of the role played by experts of the paranormal, the emphasis here being on dependency on external – supra-Self – states of affairs. We then turned to the role played by New Age expertise, the emphasis now being on the operation of her own inner spirituality or energy. And finally, we looked at Diana the expressivist, importance being attached – in this regard – to the human, the emotions, the heart.

And so to a key argument of this essay – utilising this analysis of strands in order to claim that Diana was becoming, and would have become, increasingly New Age.

Morton writes,

> '*Shortly after her retirement from public life she made a promise to herself. "I will be a puppet no longer. In the future I'm going to be true to my own beliefs and wishes', she told friends who were impressed by the sturdiness of her convictions'.*[28]

Or, as he reports the opinion of one of her 'closest advisers',

*' Diana is on a voyage of discovery at the moment. What
we are seeing is her real personality coming through because
she is no longer bound so much by the royal system. She will
make mistakes, but ultimately we will see a genuine
manifestation of the real person'.*[29]

Testimonies of this variety – and there are many – strongly suggest
that Diana's expressivistic assumptions and values served to
encourage her to rebel against the established order, most
significantly the Court, where so many fully expected her to find her
place. In tandem, so the argument goes, dissatisfaction with the
established order further encouraged interest what in her 'self' had
to offer. If one is not to be a 'puppet', if, as Morton puts it, 'one's
aim is to 'cut the strings of control', or, conversely, 'if one is acquire
control, the obvious place to look is within oneself'.[30]

But this is not all. As an expressivist, seeking liberation from
regulatory duties and role performances in order to seek inner
significance and growth, Diana was perfectly 'positioned' to enter
New Age circles. Providing a powerfully sacralised rendering of
psychological-cum-humanistic expressivism, the fact that New Age
teachings have a great deal in common with the expressive means
that it is not difficult to explain why Diana should have been
attracted by things New Age.

Looking more closely at this, we have already noted that
expressivist and New Age teachings share many values, also sharing
the three assumptions that (much) of the established, institutional
order is repressive or artificial, that truth or authenticity lies within,
and that it is possible to engage in practices to handle what is amiss
and enhance what is right. With these commonalities, it is not
surprising that Diana became more interested in what New Age
provisions had to offer. For someone already possessing ('quasi-
religious') faith in her own 'inner voice', her own self, the provisions
were plausible.[31] Furthermore, typically promising spiritual rather
than 'merely' psychological self-fulfillment, they would appear to
have been positively appealing to a person intent on taking her inner
quest yet further. The greater her distress with her 'public' life, the
argument goes, the more vital the search within: and the greater the
tendency to seek out the New Age with its quite radical (because
spiritual) promises and solutions.

In many regards, Diana's 'conversion career' is absolutely par for the course. Without going into any detail here, there is a tradition of thought – running from Georg Simmel, through Arnold Gehlen, to Peter Berger (for example) – which theorises 'the turn to the self' in terms of rebellion against the (experienced) *repressive* or 'iron cage' properties of the institutionalised mainstream of society, together with *disenchantment* with what mainstream institutions (including traditional religion) have to offer as an existential source of significance.[32] In addition, among others Berger et al have drawn attention to the fact that rebellion, disenchantment and the turn to spiritualities catering for the interests and concerns of the 'self' are closely associated with those who are *already* imbued with the expressive. (Berger et al's analysis is of the 1960s counter-culture, when numbers of younger, well-educated, middle class, people, brought up with expressive values, were prompted to pursue the spiritual quest within.[33]

Overall, for many – including Diana – involvement with the New Age is thus explicable in terms of seeing the New Age as being both a spirituality *for* modernity (handling identity problems generated by life in the mainstream) and a spirituality *of* our times (enabling people to take their expressive search within further by virtue of the fact that the New Age sacralises the more expressive aspects of culture and selfhood).[34]

In one significant regard, however, Diana is somewhat exceptional. In comparison with most of those drawn to the New Age, Diana was unusually concerned with the paranormal. (At least since her marriage, we saw earlier, she had a strong faith in astrology; and she had for long used clairvoyants to contact the dead.) Such beliefs, we can now go on to argue, made it all the more easy for her to become increasingly attracted by things New Age. That is to say, she did not have to make the conversion 'leap' – facing many – of having to come to believe in the existence of a spiritual realm: she *already* believed in it.

Her loss of faith in what the 'system' had to offer, her unhappiness with many aspects of her public, duty and role-performing life, her expressivism, her concern with herself as a – if not the – source of significance, her longstanding belief in supernatural forces and agencies: such were the concatenation of factors which propelled her towards New Age provisions. It is, of course, possible that a new life – perhaps in France – would have deflected her attention away from inner spirituality. But I doubt it. The trajectory – crudely, from rejecting van der Post to engaging with Robbins and Chopra - was increasing in strength right up to her death.

I am not suggesting that Diana would necessarily have become an 'I am God, I am God, I am God' Shirley MacLaine. But there is little doubt that the language of 'spirit' would have increasingly complemented, perhaps even supplemented, that of 'heart' - to the extent that she would have increasingly come to have been perceived as a key exemplar of the inner quest for ultimacy.

## Death, and religiosity beyond church and chapel

According to the Archbishop of Canterbury, George Carey, the 'humbling and astonishing reaction' to the death of Diana reflected a 'continuing deep respect for the Churches'.[35] In contrast to this judgment, I want to suggest that responses to her death were very much bound up with the fact that Diana had already come to serve as an exemplar of the quest within.

Insightful points, made by Jack O'Sullivan, help set the scene:

> *'[the heart] is Diana's icon, representing a devotion to feeling, compassion and emotion. But little mention of God. Diana's funeral showed post-Christian Britain out in force. Just as there was a gulf between the people and those in the Palace, the beliefs of many listening to the funeral from outside bore little resemblance to the faith of those within the church walls.*

> *People have a new religion. Most did not gather outside the Abbey and Kensington Palace to find God. They came together for a more internal exercise, to explore their all important inner selves and feelings, an event prompted by the death of a woman who excelled in expressing her own emotions.*

> *This religion is the creed of the confessional society and has been developed by a priesthood of analysts, therapists, counsellors, agony aunts and psychobabblers Its first commandment is to get in touch with your inner self. ....its individualism is essentially Protestant, about each person's relationship with him and herself. What is innovative about what is happening - let's call it New Protestantism - is its*

*secular quality, the banishment of God in favour of a spirit inside ourselves'.*[36]

Attending to O'Sullivan's 'new religion' by introducing evidence, which (unfortunately) cannot be explored in any detail here, a clear majority of the adult British population – to varying degrees and in various ways – are religious, but with little or no significant contact with either church or chapel. And of this majority it would seem that increasing numbers are interested in a religiosity or spirituality which caters for the subjectivities of the self; of what it is to be alive. Such people might very well not be explicitly New Age; but neither are they atheists or agnostics.[37]

Georg Simmel wrote that 'this emotional reality – which we can only call *life* – makes itself increasingly felt in its formless strength as the true meaning or value of our existence'. As he also argued, 'the turn to the self means that when people are (so-to-speak) left to themselves, dwell on themselves and have to rely on their own resources to make sense of their lives, we find a 'spiritual reality' to do with the 'the self-consciousness of the metaphysical significance of our existence'.[38]

If this is correct, many peoples' 'religion' is an (often inchoate, ill-articulated) sense that (their) *life*, the depths of what it is to *be*, transcends the mundane, the secular, the realm of bodies and brains. And if this is indeed the case, then Diana's life – with all the reports of her quest within, her concern with the authentically human – served as a perfect exemplar: an exemplar which fully came into its own with the shocking realisation that *life* – with all its value – yet dies. Hence so much of the grief, the mourning.

Morton is surely on the right lines when he concludes *Diana, Her True Story - In Her Own Words* by suggesting that 'much of her attraction lay in the way she tapped into a spiritual undercurrent in society'.[39] More exactly, however, I think that it can be argued that from the point of view of national appeal, death came at precisely the right time. If Diana had lived, to continue becoming more and more obviously 'alternative' or New Age, the strong suspicion is that she would increasingly have been perceived as 'whacky', with only New Agers themselves taking her seriously. The fact that her conversion career was terminated by her death, however, meant that her 'heart' was not seen as too out-of-the-ordinary, too weird. Suffused with enough 'spirituality' or 'depth' to lend it aura, her way of 'being' could thus resonate with all those who sense that 'spirituality' - albeit inchoately - lies at the core of what it is to be human.

## Spiritual shopping, and cultural elites

In the main, this essay has dwelt on Diana's own life, more general considerations having entered the picture only with regard to what has attracted people to the New Age Movement and to diagnosing the cultural significance of Diana's death. It remains to draw attention to two other matters of broader significance.

The first concerns Diana and her 'spiritual shopping'. Just as in many regards Diana exemplifies an important strain of religiosity beyond church and chapel (and, to some extent, within these institutions), so, too, do her activities serve to exemplify an important way of engaging with what is on offer. As was noted at the beginning of this essay, Diana drew on a range of experts, some concentrating on her past, others the present, yet others the future; some teaching spirituality, others of a humanistic or secular orientation. The term 'shopping' is in order in this regard in that she would look around, select particular provisions according to her specific requirements, move from one 'outlet' to another if she was not satisfied, and would have (at least expected) to pay for the 'services'.

Many have noted that the *bricoleur* is an increasingly important figure of our culture.[40] As the term implies, what matters is having things work, drawing on resources to get results. Pragmatic considerations overrule matters to do with conceptual coherence. And Diana the *bricoleur* illustrates this well. Rather than attempting to construct her own, logically coherent, set of beliefs, assumptions and values, she drew on whatever was required for the task at hand. It might be illogical to turn to an astrologer one day (emphasising dependency), a New Age teacher the next (emphasising self-responsibility); a practitioner of inner spirituality, then a 'secular' therapist; a guru dwelling on the challenges of the search within, then someone providing consumeristic, 'pamper Diana days'.[41] But this is beside the point if one's pressing aim is to handle different aspects of one's life in a *functionally* efficacious - and hopefully *functionally* coherent - manner.

Our second, concluding topic concerns the operation of New Age and other alternative teachings among cultural elites. On first sight, one might think that Diana was exceptional. Far from it. The

Royal Family itself is steeped in the alternative: the Queen, the Queen Mother, the Princess Royal, indeed most senior members of the family, with their faith in complementary/alternative medicine; Sarah and her involvement with spiritual adviser Vasso Kortesis; and, above all, Prince Charles informed by what Jonathan Dimbleby describes as 'an inner alliance of his own intuition with a faith in the immanence of a non-denominational human spirit', his major guru having been van der Post with his claim, for example, that 'If you can keep in contact with the Great Memory, which is reached through instinct and intuition, you can come a long way. It is never wrong'.[42]

Indeed, it is not an exaggeration to say that many of the variations on the theme of inner spirituality have been played out within Royal circles: healing, nature 'religion', the 'religion' of humanity, the arts, the quest for prosperity, even pleasure.

As for other cultural elites, one might think of presidents (Mitterrand with his astrologer, Elisabeth Teissier; Clinton with his Mexican shaman Salvador Lunes Collazo); other political figures (Hillary Clinton 'docking with one's angel' with New Age Jean Houston; William Hague and Transcendental Meditation); film stars galore (for example Madonna, Elizabeth Taylor and the Kabbalah); TV personalities (Oprah Winfrey and 'my divine self'); members of high society (Maurizio Gucci with his white witch; Patrizia Gucci with her clairvoyant Pina Auriemma); even football managers (Croatian coach Miroslav Blazevic and Aston Villa's John Gregory, with their astrologers).

To date, this territory remains ill-explored by academics. Of particular note, it would be extremely interesting to look at whether or not involvement with alternative beliefs and practices makes a difference to the lives of members of cultural elites; and, if the answer is in the affirmative, to ascertain what kind of difference is in evidence. To close with one thought on this matter, it is pretty clear that Diana's expressivism, together with her questing within for spirituality, played a major role in her (in effect) leaving the Royal Family. What she found critically important - fully engaging with negative emotions to deal with them; 'awakening' herself; seeking the truth of others - clashed with the dominant values of the Royal system: the repetition of tradition; the control, distance, formality, hierarchy, reserve, duty, self-sacrifice. In contrast, however, Charles has found ways of 'marrying' his - more 'philosophical', less 'psychological' - inner quest with what he values about tradition. Ironically, at the time of her death, Diana might have been spiritually closer to Charles than ever before, but whereas her inner quest exacerbated tensions with the Royal 'system', Charles' has come to inform his role as the leading Royal 'guru'.

# References

1  Diana, cited in Andrew Morton, *Diana, Her New Life*, London, Michael O'Mara Books Limited, 1995, p. 155.
2  Morton: *Diana, Her New Life*.
3  Michael Perry, *Gods Within*, London, SPCK, 1992, p. 147; my emphasis.
4  For a considerably more comprehensive account of the characteristics of the New Age Movement, see Paul Heelas, *The New Age Movement. The Celebration of the Self and the Sacralisation of Modernity*, Oxford, Blackwell, 1996. See especially chapter 1, 'Manifestations'.
5  Morton, *Diana, Her New Life*; Andrew Morton, *Diana, Her True Story - In Her Own Words*, London, Michael O'Mara, 1997; Julie Birchill, *Diana*, London, Weidenfeld & Nicolson, 1998; Beatrix Campbell, *Diana, Princess of Wales. How Sexual Politics Shook the Monarchy*, London, The Women's Press, 1998.
6  Campbell, *Diana*, p. 173.
7  Morton, *Diana, Her New Life*, pp. 15; 109; 101; 118-9.
8  Morton, *Diana, Her New Life*, p. 84; see also the 'great store' she placed in a forecast that 1993 was going to be a terrible year (p. 70).
9  Morton, *Diana, Her New Life*, pp. 84; 88; 103; my emphasis.
10  See the *Sunday Mirror*, 18 January 1998; *The Sun* 12 August 1997.
11  This is not to say, however, that astrology (etc.) cannot be incorporated in the New Age frame of reference - as when, for example, astrology is deployed as a tool to help diagnose why one's life is not working. But although there are signs of this in Diana's usage (see, for example, Morton, *Diana, Her True Story*, p. 163), it is not to the fore.
12  Cited by Morton, *Diana, Her True Story*, p. 43.
13  Anthony Robbins, *Unlimited Power. The New Science of Personal Achievement*, London, Simon & Schuster, 1988.
14  Robbins: *Unlimited Power*, pp. 248; 320; 337; 348.
15  Anna Pasternak, 'Soul Searching', *The Sunday Times* (Style), pp. 33-4.
16  Morton: *Diana, Her True Story*, p. 64; my emphasis.
17  Morton: *Diana, Her New Life*: pp. 60-61; astrologer Felix Lyle is cited by Morton: *Diana, Her True Story*, p. 208.
18  MacLaine, as cited by Heelas: *The New Age Movement*, p. 1.
19  Edward Shils, *Tradition*, London, Faber and Faber, pp. 10-11. See also Charles Taylor, *The Ethics of Authenticity*, London, Harvard University Press, 1991, eg. pp. 14; 26; 27; 29; 61.
20  For a transcript of the *Panorama* interview, see *The Daily Telegraph*, 21 November 1995, pp. 2-4.

21  Morton: *Diana, Her True Story*, pp. 34, 255, 62; my emphases.
22  Morton: *Diana, Her New Life*, p. 152.
23  Morton: *Diana, Her New Life*, respectively, p. 66; p. 89; p. 90; p. 123; p. 124; p. 65; p. 94; see also Morton: *Diana, Her True Story*, a friend reporting, 'she understands the essence of people, what a person is about rather than who they are' (p. 208).
24  See the transcript in *The Daily Telegraph*, 21 November 1995, pp. 2-4.
25  See Robert Hardman, 'Princess Embraces the Commonwealth', *The Daily Telegraph*, 2 November 1996, p. 8.
26  Morton: *Diana, Her New Life*, p. 156 (on 'the temple of her body'); p. 14.
27  The term 'conversion career' is taken from the title of *Conversion Careers*, James Richardson (ed.), (London, Sage, 1977).
28  Morton: *Diana, Her New Life*, p. 121.
29  Morton: *Diana, Her New Life*, p. 91.
30  Morton: *Diana, Her New Life*, p. 89.
31  On expressivism as 'quasi-religious' see Paul Heelas, 'Expressive Spirituality and Humanistic Expressivism: Sources of Significance beyond Church and Chapel', in Steven Sutcliffe and Marion Bowman (eds), *Beyond the New Age: Alternative Spirituality in Britain*, Edinburgh, Edinburgh University Press, 1999.
32  Georg Simmel, The Future of Our Culture', in P. A. Lawrence, *Georg Simmel. Sociologist and European*, Middlesex, Thomas Nelson, 1976, pp. 250-2; Arnold Gehlen, *Man in the Age of Technology* New York, Columbia University Press, 1980; Peter Berger, *The Heretical Imperative*, New York, Doubleday, 1979.
33  See Peter Berger, Brigitte Berger and Hansfried Kellner, *The Homeless Mind*, Harmondsworth, Penguin, 1974.
34  See Heelas: *The New Age Movement*, especially chapters 5 and 6. In passing, it can be noted that the (experienced) 'deconstruction' of selfhood with regard to the public realm of mainstream, institutionalised identity provisions does not mean that those turning within are postmodern: at least to the extent that their quest is for the essential; the foundational; the *ens realissium*.
35  Cited by Victoria Combe, 'Carey tells of Lessons from Grief over Diana', *The Daily Telegraph*, 14 October 1997.
36  Jack O'Sullivan, 'Diana's Devotees join the New Religion', *The Independent*, 8 September 1997.
37  For a more detailed account, see Heelas: 'Expressive Spirituality'. A systematic study of young people, largely beyond church and chapel, whose 'immanent faith structure' is of an immanent, personal, self-orientated variety, is provided by Sylvia Collins' *Young People's Faith in Late Modernity*, Unpublished PhD, University of Surrey, 1997. Compare Grace Davie, *Religion in Britain since 1945. Believing Without Belonging*, Oxford, Blackwell, 1994 for a more Christian-orientated reading of what is taking place beyond church and chapel.
38  Georg Simmel, 'The Conflict of Modern Culture, in Georg Simmel,

*Essays on Religion*, New Haven and London, Yale University Press, 1997, pp. 20-25, p. 24; Georg Simmel, The Problem of Religion today, in Georg Simmel, *Essays on Religion*, New Haven and London, Yale University Press, 1997, pp. 7-19, p. 18.

39  Morton: *Diana, Her True Story*, p. 283.

40  See, for example, Robert Wuthnow's suggestion that 'the religion practised by an increasing number of Americans may be entirely their own manufacture - a kind of eclectic synthesis of Christianity, popular psychology, Reader's Digest folklore, and personal superstitions, all wrapped up in the anecdotes of the individual's biography'. *The Struggle for America's Soul. Evangelicals, Liberals, and Secularism*, Michigan, William B. Eerdmans, 1989, pp. 116-17.

41  Diana herself used the term ' Pamper Diana' days. See Morton: *Diana, Her True Story*, p. 231.

42  Respectively, see Robert Hardman, 'Prince Pioneers Alternative Option', *The Daily Telegraph* 21 October 1997, p. 13; Vasso Kortesis, *The Duchess of York Uncensored*, London, Blake Publishing, 1996; p. 255; Jonathan Dimbleby, *The Prince of Wales. A Biography*, London, Little, Brown and Company, 1994, p. 255; Angela Levin, 'What Charles's Guru thinks about that Diana Interview', the *Daily Mail* 29 November 1995, p. 27. See also Morton: *Diana, Her True Story*, p. 163, on the claim that 'numerous members of the Royal family, including the Queen Mother, the Queen and Prince Philip have attended seances and other investigations into the paranormal'.

# 6. Diana and the Religion of the Heart

## Linda Woodhead

*The nation has found its heart*

(Message on a floral tribute at Kensington Palace)

*Diana, God blessed you with faith, hope, charity and love.*
*RIP*

(Jones Bircotes, Doncaster, a message in *Diana. The People's Pictures*, *Sun* newspapers special tribute, 21 August, 1998)

*The Diana Effect:*

*Charity donations up,*

*Crime down,*

*Little acts of kindness on the increase.*

(*Now* magazine, front cover, 2 November, 1997)

Shortly after Diana's death, the bishops of the Church of England met to discuss her religious significance. One of their conclusions, the *Church Times* reported, was that the extraordinary reaction to Diana's death was a sign of the vast reserves of 'implicit religion' lurking just below the surface of contemporary life.[1] This statement, like some other recent Church reports, begs a crucial question: just which religion is implicit? In what follows, I shall suggest that we need to be cautious about assuming that it is Christianity. What I hope to show is that the religion which Diana articulated through her words and her deeds, and the religion which seems to have resonated with so many of those who mourned her, was perfectly explicit, and that although it owed a debt to Christianity, it was not Christian in any traditional sense. By paying closer attention to statements by Diana and her admirers, it is possible to discern the outlines of this religion, a religion more widespread in contemporary society than is often recognised, and a religion superbly adapted to life in late modernity. It could be called a 'Religion of Tender Loving Care', or a 'Religion of Tender-Hearted Humanitarianism', but Diana's own words suggest instead the simpler 'Religion of the Heart'.

## The Princess and the Nun

The convergencies and divergences between the religion of the heart and more traditional forms of Christianity can be well illustrated by a comparison between the Princess and Mother Teresa. The affinity between by the two women is well known. Mother Teresa is reported to have said that the Princess of Wales 'is like a daughter to me'; Diana's desk at Kensington Palace was adorned by a statue of Christ draped with rosaries given her by the Pope and Mother Teresa.[2] Some of the most famous of all the Diana pictures show the two women gazing at one another with evident satisfaction and mutual admiration. The grounds for their mutual respect are obvious. Both Diana and Mother Teresa were among a handful of women of the late twentieth century to achieve international celebrity status. They occupied traditional roles (nun, wife, mother and princess), but subverted and transformed them in ways which enabled them to become the basis of careers of considerable fame and power. Finally and most importantly, both women were celebrated for their humanitarian work: 'Although differing in age, these two women represent humanitarian spirit and generosity', as the caption under a picture of the two puts it.[3]

It is quite obvious, however, that neither Diana nor Mother Teresa were humanitarians in any secular sense. Both saw their humanitarian work as part of a wider religious mission, and both were inspired by what may be called religions of love. Thus both explain their public work in terms of the need to show love to those who are suffering or unloved. The commandment to love, Mother Teresa insisted, is the greatest of all commandments; the state of being unloved the greatest poverty of all:

> *'You have a welfare state in England, but I have walked at night and gone into your homes and found people dying*

*unloved. Here you have a different kind of poverty – a*
*poverty of spirit, of loneliness, and of being unwanted'.*[4]

Initially made famous by her home for the dying in Calcutta, Mother
Teresa's purpose was not to cure its inmates but to show them that
'there are people who really love them'.[5] Diana would manifest
similar compassion for the terminally ill. Like Mother Teresa too,
the Princess went on to develop a concern for the homeless, for AIDS
victims, and for needy children.

In these ways then, Diana shared with Mother Teresa a religion
of love and of the heart. It is no coincidence that Mother Teresa
called her home for the dying *'Nirmal Hriday'*: 'Pure Heart'. Yet the
name hints at a significant difference between Diana's Religion of
the Heart and Mother Teresa's Catholicism. In Christian
understanding, the pure in heart are those who keep themselves free
from other distractions in order to serve God with total dedication.
In Mother Teresa's monastic brand of Christianity such distractions
include wealth, luxury, sex and sensuality, and any wilful assertion
of self. The vows of poverty, chastity and obedience which she and
her Sisters of Mercy took were their antidotes. As Mother Teresa
explained,

> *"I will be a saint" means I will despoil myself of all that is*
> *not God; I will strip my heart of all created things; I will*
> *live in poverty and detachment; I will renounce my will, my*
> *inclinations, my whims and fancies, and make myself a*
> *willing slave to the will of God'.*[6]

In this quest for purity, in her prayer that her Sisters might 'live in
the world as the brides of Jesus, neither belonging to the world nor
following its corrupt ways', Mother Teresa makes clear her considerable distance from Diana. Even if one does not believe Lady Colin
Campbell's breathless account of just how many 'hunky and chunky'
lovers Diana took before, during and after her marriage to Charles, it
is clear that chastity did not hold quite the same exalted place in
Diana's moral scheme as in Mother Teresa's.[7] The same, of course,
could be said of the Princess in relation to the virtues of poverty and
obedience.

These differences between Diana and Mother Teresa seem to
be symptoms of an even deeper difference which takes us to the heart

of their religious visions. Whereas Diana's vision (it will be argued below) was focused firmly on the sacredness of the human, Mother Teresa's vision was centred on a transcendent God incarnate in Jesus Christ. In this sense, Mother Teresa's religion was (as Diana's was not) a 'religion of difference', a religion which stressed not the continuity, but the distance between the human and the divine – between creator and created, infinite and finite, perfect God and sinful humanity. Where Diana looked within to find God, Mother Teresa looked up; where Diana saw human loveliness, Mother Teresa saw sinful humanity; and where Diana saw uniquely valuable human beings, Mother Teresa saw Christ.

The Christocentrism of Mother Teresa's religion was unmistakable. Christ, she believed, was the one who inspired all her thoughts and actions. In the true saint, individual volition must give way to Christ so that Christ may work through the human. As she said, 'The Work is [Christ's] work and will remain so, all of us are but his instruments, who do our little bit and pass by.'[8] Likewise, the proper object of Christian love, in Mother Teresa's view, was nothing but Christ himself. So she spoke not of loving the poor for their own sakes or because of their inherent loveliness, but of loving Christ in the poor. What is important, she says, is 'to look at them as Christ', and 'to see Christ in them'. For 'Christ is working with us and through us in the poor and for the poor.'[9] The following exchange with Malcolm Muggeridge makes her position plain:

### MOTHER TERESA

*Because we cannot see Christ we cannot express our love to him; but our neighbours we can always see, and we can do to them what if we saw him we would like to do to Christ.*

### MALCOLM

*You don't think there's a danger that people might mistake the means for the end, and feel that serving their fellow men was an end in itself. Do you think there's a danger in that?*

### MOTHER TERESA

*There is always the danger that we may become only social workers, or do the work for the sake of the work... Our works are only an expression of our love for Christ.*[10]

In Mother Teresa's moral economy, in other words, self and other must both be effaced to make way for Christ. Love consists not in one loving and lovable human being loving another, but in sinful creatures effacing their own reality so that they may become channels through whom God may love Himself. In expressing these views, Mother Teresa is giving voice to a well established interpretation of Christian love, an interpretation given theological voice in the twentieth century by Anders Nygren in his book *Agape and Eros*, and popularised by C.S. Lewis in *The Four Loves*. The effect of both books was to draw a clear line between a self-sacrificing divine love ('agape'), and more selfish forms of human love. The ideal has also been kept alive through Christian teaching, preaching and hagiography. As a pupil in a Roman Catholic convent in England in the Seventies, for example, I can myself well remember the pervasiveness of this ideal of selfless love, an ideal held before us by the example of the saints, particularly female saints. In naming herself after one of the most celebrated of these self-denying saints, St Thérèse of Lisieux, Mother Teresa demonstrates her allegiance to the ideal. As we shall see, it was an ideal rather different from that which Diana came to embrace and to embody in the 'new life' which she forged after her separation from Charles.

## Diana's Relations with Institutional Christianity

The widely circulated pictures of a demure Diana veiled in black standing before Pope John Paul II in 1985 led to persistent rumours that she was thinking of converting to the Roman Catholic church. The speculation increased after her divorce. Not only had the Duchess of Kent and Diana's mother converted, but Diana was known to have been talking with senior clerics in the Catholic church. At one point the speculation was so intense that a concerned senior Tory was moved to ask constitutional experts whether Charles would be able to become King if his separated wife were a Roman Catholic.[11]

Diana may have enjoyed the discomfort she caused by showing an interest in the Roman Catholic church. There is little evidence, however, that she seriously intended to convert to Catholicism – or to any other form of institutional Christianity for that matter. She described her first audience with the Pope as a somewhat uncomfortable meeting with 'this man in a white frock', and in later life commented that 'I've about as much chance of becoming a Buddhist or becoming a Muslim as converting to Catholicism'.[12] On the contrary, the available evidence (admittedly slim) suggests Diana's profound ambivalence towards those traditional, institutional forms of Christianity which Ernst Troeltsch classified as the 'church' type.[13]

This ambivalence certainly extended to the Anglicanism into which Diana was born and to which her marriage tied her even more closely. Though his relations with Diana were largely confined to the early days of her marriage, Robert Runcie's comments about Diana, Charles and the Church of England, recorded in Humphrey Carpenter's biography, are revealing. Charles, Runcie famously complained, had grown distant from Anglicanism. Despite his early formation by Michael Ramsey and his *Spectator*-like talk about 'the lovely language of the Prayer Book', any genuine love and care for the the Church of England on the Prince's part 'had passed away'. The Prince, Runcie observed, was 'a mass of confusions', and nowhere more so than in relation to religion: 'He's on about the grandeur of our cathedrals and the epic language of the Prayer Book, but he wants to be exploring Hinduism with people in the inner cities', said Runcie. He was 'deeply into the Laurens van der Post spirituality', but, like the Queen, was also a person 'of formal personal piety': they are 'people who intercede, who say their nightly prayers'.[14]

When things began to go wrong in his marriage, Charles appealed to Runcie on the basis that (in Runcie's words) 'It's been rather a lot for Diana, because religion hasn't stuck much with her. And we feel we ought to mention it to you, because you married us'.[15] (Charles had also called upon Laurens van der Post for help in this trying matter.) The Archbishop was commissioned to meet regularly with Diana. What she needed, Charles thought, was 'a bit of instruction'. But what Diana really needed, Runcie believed, was not instruction but encouragement:

> 'When you began on abstract ideas, you could see her eyes clouding over, her eyelids become heavy ... And yet she had a sort of shrewdness, and was tremendously observant ... she came to Canterbury once, and she wrote to somebody and said she'd been to lunch with me, and she said, "Guess what, we had grilled sole!"'[16]

However obliquely, these remarks reveal something of significance about how Diana's attitude to the Church of England may have developed. The sequence of events recounted by Runcie seems likely to have confirmed in Diana the view that his brand of Christianity a) had more to do with ideas than with people and b) was part and parcel of the 'establishment' which included the Royal Family, her husband, and their courtiers. As Diana increasingly came to view the latter as an external and oppressive cage in which she was trapped, it seems likely that Anglicanism – together with other forms of church Christianity – became tarred for her with the same brush. A number of Diana's subsequent remarks reveal how, as she matured, gained in self-confidence, and cut herself loose from her marriage to Charles and her obligations to the Royal Family, the Princess gradually came to distinguish quite clearly between a religion of free spirits on the one hand, and of institutional restriction on the other. Where the former was concerned with persons, the latter was concerned with ideas; where the former was directly open to the spiritual realm, the latter was concerned with ritual and dogma; where the former had to do with inner matters, the latter had to do with externals; where the former was spontaneous, natural and honest, the latter was dry, artificial and superficial; where the former was concerned with the present, the latter was concerned with tradition and with the past; and where the former was autonomous and liberating, the latter was heteronomous and restrictive.

Interestingly, Diana's frankest views on these matters are probably captured on the so-called 'Squidgy' Tapes, the recording of a 'phone conversation between her and James Gilbey which is now thought to have been made and deliberately broadcast by the secret services in order that a member of the public might intercept and release it (as did indeed happen).[17] In the midst of an intimate late-night conversation, Diana recalls an encounter with 'that bloody bishop', the Bishop of Norwich:

> DIANA
>
> *He said, "I want you to tell me how you talk to people who are ill or dying. How do you cope?"*
>
> JAMES
>
> *He wanted to learn. He was so hopeless at it himself.*
>
> DIANA
>
> *I began to wonder after I'd spoken to him. I said, "I'm just*

*myself"... In the end I said, "I know this sounds crazy, but
I've lived before". He said, "How do you know?" I said,
"Because I'm a wise old thing"... I said, "Also, I'm aware
that people I have loved and have died and are in the spirit
world look after me". He looked horrified. I thought, "If he's
the bishop, he should say that sort of thing"... I said, "I
understand people's suffering, people's pain, more than you
will ever know". And he said, "That's obvious by what you
are doing for AIDS". I said, "It's not only AIDS, it's
anyone who suffers. I can smell them a mile away".*

*JAMES*

*What did he say?*

*DIANA*

*Nothing. He just went quiet. He changed the subject to toys.
And I thought, "Ah! Defeated you".*[18]

The conversation is enormously revealing of Diana's attitude to
Anglicanism, and probably to organised religion in general. Religion,
she clearly believes, is something instinctive not something learned
(not a matter of 'instruction'). Thus she cannot explain to the bishop
how she talks to the ill and dying: she is just herself. Likewise, the
content of religion for Diana clearly has nothing to do with doctrine
or belief, but is a matter of loving action, of caring for people. Diana
appears to feel superior to this dignitary of the Church because he
seems to have no direct experience of spiritual matters. By contrast,
Diana sees herself as spiritually intuitive in a way the Bishop is not.
He may preach about religion, but Diana knows at first hand. She
has connections with the spirit world, and with those who are suffering in this world. As such, she is a rival for the bishop; she has
'defeated' him on his own territory.

Diana, in other words, did not simply dismiss Christianity out
of hand. The whole thrust of this exchange with the bishop is not
that she is rejecting Christianity nor proposing an alternative religion,
but that she is claiming to be a better Christian than the Church's
official representative. Yet in interpreting true Christianity as a
matter of direct spiritual intuition and of direct action in caring for
others, she is nonetheless proposing a Christianity which is
significantly different from the traditional forms of 'mainline'

Christianity, both Anglican and Catholic, with which she had some connection. Here again the differences explored in relation to Mother Teresa come into sharp focus, and here again we see why there was probably never any real danger of Diana's joining the Roman Catholic church. Mother Teresa embraced and supported the institutional church in a way Diana never could. Despite her undoubted determination and shrewdness, Mother Teresa was proud of the fact that she never did anything outside the discipline of the church or without the approval of her (male) clerical superiors. She saw herself not as independent, but as obedient. She loved the church, and believed in the supernatural power of its sacraments: the Mass, she said, 'is the spiritual food that sustains me, without which I could not get through one single day or hour in my life'.[19] Likewise, Mother Teresa was a feisty supporter of the Church's teaching, and a tireless campaigner against abortion and contraception. She was, so to speak, the Pope's right hand man.[20]

By contrast, Diana's experiences within the bosom of the Royal Family left her deeply hostile towards established and powerful institutions, and towards the men who upheld them. In Diana's scheme of things, it was not institutions which were important, but individual human beings and their feelings. It was the heart that mattered.

## Diana's Religion of the Heart

Diana's disillusionment with institutional Christianity did not lead to a more general disillusionment with religion. On the contrary, her attempt to forge a new life independent of Charles and the Royal Family led her to develop her 'spiritual side' more than ever before. As Andrew Morton's *Diana: Her New Life* makes clear, Diana viewed this spiritual growth as one of her most important achievements, and she articulated her new sense of mission and purpose in explicitly spiritual terms.

The claim that the religion which Diana articulated in the last years of her life was increasingly New Age (a claim made by Paul Heelas within this volume) finds some strong grounds for support. As Heelas points out, Diana increasingly relied on the services of a very wide range of New Age and 'expressive' trainers, counsellors and therapists, and willingly embraced an expressive discourse of being true to self, loving self, and finding the 'real me'.[21] Yet Diana never focused upon such goals to the exclusion of her other great concern: the giving of love to others. Or, to put it more accurately, she never saw the two goals as mutually exclusive. On the contrary, she believed that they informed one another. It was necessary to love self in order to love others; it was necessary to love others – and to be loved by others – in order to fulfil self. Diana's Religion of the Heart was not simply a religion of self: it was a religion of loving kindness directed to all needy human beings, self *and* others. It could be said that it drew on Christianity insofar as it stressed the importance of love and service to others, and on more expressive influences insofar as it stressed the importance of self.

In its synthesis of these different influences, the Religion of the Heart moved beyond both. In relation to Christianity this is beautifully illustrated by the epitaph quoted at the start of this essay in which an admirer speaks of Diana as blessed with 'faith, hope, charity *and love*'. The heretical addition of 'love' to the traditional trinity of Christian virtues reveals that Diana is here thought of not just as an exemplary Christian, but as adding something extra. As this and other examples of contemporary talk about charity reveal, the latter has come to be identified with the benevolent and beneficent distribution of largesse to those less fortunate than oneself. It is the sort of thing which a Mother Teresa, a bishop (or a prince) exemplifies, a matter of doing good to others. For the Religion of the Heart, this may be admirable, but it is not enough. What is additionally required is a love which is warmer, more emotional, tender and reciprocal – a love like Diana's.

The affective nature of this 'heart love' is one of its most important distinguishing marks. It has little to do with the head, and even less to do with rules or with duty. It is something 'inner' rather than external. Diana's stress on the importance of feelings is well known, and was often intended as a contrast to the 'repressed' Royal Family. In relation to her boys, for example, her approach was to 'hug my children to death. I get into bed with them at night and say "Who loves you most in the whole world?" and they always say "Mummy". I feed them love and affection – it's so important'.[22]

In spite of the charge that such emotivism tends to be subjectivist and quietist, Diana's Religion of the Heart proved surprisingly subversive. An ethic of duty and self-sacrifice was part and parcel of an established Anglicanism which has for at least three centuries legitimated an aristocratic social order in Britain. It teaches that virtue consists in obedience to higher powers, both religious and social. By contrast, Diana's Religion of the Heart encouraged spiritual independence and individual empowerment, and inspired Diana in her struggles against 'the Establishment'. It also turned her lack of learning and educational accomplishment into a positive virtue. Where Charles favoured a religion based on a mix of Prayer Book Anglicanism and the books of Laurens van der Post, Diana depended on nothing more than intuition, feeling, and a sense of spiritual connection with others. The latter, of course, are qualities to which anyone can lay claim, irrespective of class, education, or gender. Historically, they have proved particularly congenial to women who have always played a preponderant role in the mystical, affective strands of religion, probably because of their exclusion from institutions of learning and clerical power.

Whilst the Religion of the Heart may thus be uncongenial to cultural and social elites, it has an obvious appeal to those who feel themselves marginal to such elites (of whom even a Princess could be one). Its egalitarian dynamics were also played out in its reinterpretation of Christian charity. As some critics of Mother Teresa have noted, the latter is often implicitly hierarchical. Its model is of an invulnerable giver (God, the saint), dispensing grace to an undeserving recipient (sinful humanity). In a colonial context, this can easily support the idea of the White Man's Burden of care for the helpless native. By contrast, the Religion of the Heart favours a love which is mutual and equal. Where Mother Teresa was generally pictured ministering to dependent black people, Diana grew wary of such images. When in 1993, for example, she was made to take a photocall in Zimbabwe doling out food to children, she protested that it patronised the children, humiliated her, and reinforced the 'begging-bowl' image of Africa.[23] Similarly, Diana never adopted Mother Teresa's discourse of 'the poor', with its implication that the world can be divided into givers and recipients. Speaking of her desire to help ordinary people, 'the man on the street', Diana struggled for words: 'I hate saying "man on the street" – it sounds so condescending'.[24]

In a departure from the traditional Christian model of charity too, Diana was not afraid to admit her own fallibility and neediness. She readily admitted that she received from those she met as much as she gave. As she said in her *Panorama* interview, 'in a way, by being out in public they [the public] supported me, although they weren't aware just how much healing they were giving me, and it carried me through'. As television footage reveals, Diana tried to meet people at their own level – literally as well as metaphorically. She talked about soap operas, her own problems, her own feelings: 'I say, "did you see so-and-so"? "Wasn't it funny when this happened or that happened"? and you are immediately on the same level. You are not the princess and the general public – it's the same level'.[25] Neither Diana nor the religion she sought to embody placed much weight on saintliness nor on any other form of religio-social differentiation, and she was always at pains to insist that she was no saint. Yet it seems to have been precisely her willingness to admit failures, embarrassments, vulnerability and humiliations which made many people love, admire and even revere her. As a message on a card at Kensington Palace put it:

*Saint DIANA*

*THE IRREPLACEABLE PATRON SAINT OF LOVE*

*In Our Hearts Forever.*[26]

When Basil Hume felt compelled to insist on the greater sanctity of Mother Teresa than of Diana, he therefore highlighted how far the popular understanding of sanctity had departed from a traditional Christian understanding.[27] The saint revered by the Religion of the Heart was ordinary rather than extraordinary, and loving rather than charitable. As Lady Colin Campbell summed up the sentiment in relation to Diana: 'She did not need perfection. She had humanity'.[28]

Campbell's words also serve to remind us of the importance of the language of humanity and humanitarianism to the Religion of the Heart, and language which Diana herself often used. In the BBC documentary filmed during her visit to mine victims in Angola early in 1997, for example, she said,:

> *'I am not a political figure, nor do I want to be one. But I come with my heart, and I want to bring awareness to people in distress, whether it's in Angola or in any other part of the world. The fact is, I'm a humanitarian figure. I always have been, and I always will be'.*[29]

One of the salient features of humanitarian discourse has always been its universalism: as a universal category 'the human' transcends all differences, enabling humanitarians to affirm a mission in which each individual has equal claim. Diana's Religion of the Heart certainly adopted such universalism, and in doing so revealed another cultural debt: to the Enlightenment and to liberal Christianity.[30] In addition, however, the Religion of the Heart adopted a newer form of universalism, a universalism which refuses to recognise a distinction between different *types* of love (such as 'eros' and 'agape', for example). For the Religion of the Heart, there is only one form of love: the affective, engaged, reciprocal love outlined above. It is this same love which is displayed in friendship, in romance, in parenthood, in compassionate care, in religious devotion. Love is one, though it may have different objects. Since its touchstone is intensity of feeling, its most sublime form is generally taken to be romantic and erotic love. This was certainly true for Diana, but what is equally true is that she drew no hard and fast distinction between such love and the love she felt for those outside her intimate circle. The effect, of course, was not only to universalise the ideal of intimate love, but to domesticate the ideal of benevolent love.

It is also to the discourse and conceptuality of humanitarianism that we must look in order to understand something of the metaphysical dimension of the Religion of the Heart. For, unlike traditional Christianity, such religion finds its ontological basis not so much in God as in the human. Where Christianity finds wilful and sinful creatures who are loved by God in spite of their sinfulness, the Religion of the Heart finds a uniquely precious individual who is inherently lovable. Where Christianity postulates original sin, the Religion of the Heart postulates original goodness. The latter admits that society and circumstance may lead these lovable beings astray, but maintains that they have only to return to their true selves in order to be saved, and that the experience of loving and being loved is integral and indispensable to this process.

For all its emphasis on the human, however, the Religion of the Heart does not necessarily shun belief in God. In its more Christian forms, for example, God may be seen as the originator of human value. Yet even in these forms, something of the reality and the value of the divine is transferred to the human. It is as if the human becomes brighter at the same time that the divine loses something of its radiance. Characteristics traditionally attributed to God begin to float across to the human. Instead of being understood as an Earth-bound mortal creature of dust and ashes, the human becomes a spiritual being with supernatural capabilities. As we have seen, Diana herself maintained these beliefs strongly. Some remarks included in Morton's *Diana, Her True Story in Her Own Words* are revealing:

> 'She [the late Countess Spencer] looks after me in the spirit
> world. I know that for a fact... She was sweet and
> wonderful and special. Divine really... I've got a lot of that
> [déjà vu]. Places I think I've been before, people I've never
> met. I've known her [Debbie Frank, her astrologer] for
> about three years... She does astrology and counselling...
> with astrology I listen to it but I don't believe it totally. It's
> a direction and a suggestion rather than it's definitely going
> to happen... [on a visit to her clairvoyant] My
> grandmother came in first, very strong, then my uncle and
> then Barry [Mannakee]..'.[31]

For Diana, in other words, the line between the supernatural and the natural, the human and divine was blurred. So real has the human become to the Religion of the Heart that it can no longer be defeated by death, but endures beyond the grave in a realm which is still often referred to as 'heaven'. Interestingly though, this is no longer a heaven with gates. In keeping with the cultural logic of the Religion of the Heart, admittance is universal and judgment has disappeared. Human beings do not need to undergo examination in order to enter into a divine inheritance which is theirs by nature and by right.

## Significance

This account of Diana's Religion of the Heart leaves open two vital questions: does it merit the title 'religion' at all?; and how extensive is its influence? Only empirical research can satisfactorily answer the last question, and few studies have yet been undertaken which have a direct bearing on the question. In their absence, the extraordinary response to Diana's life and death may itself offer a few clues – in relation to Britain at least.

The first question is more easily answered. If our model of what counts as religion is shaped by traditional, institutional forms of Christianity, then it is certainly doubtful whether Diana's Religion of the Heart counts as a religion. Some of the most important ways in which it differs from the church type of Christianity have been reviewed above. On the other hand, we have seen how easily the Religion of the Heart accepts, assimilates and appropriates many Christian teachings – even though their meaning and significance may be radically reinterpreted in the process. Also, as we will see in a moment, adherents of the Religion of the Heart are certainly present within Christian churches as well as outside. (They are also present in other religions, not least in Hinduism, though sadly there is no time to explore this subject here.)

The argument that Diana's Religion of the Heart does not count as real religion tends then to be predicated on belief that traditional, conservative, and orthodox forms of institutional Christianity provide the blueprint for what counts as religion. A recent article by the church historian and theologian, Edward Norman, illustrates this point of view. Norman describes Diana's religiosity as,

> 'the secularised love of humanity which is the modern substitute for religion ... it is a religion of empty sentiment, without doctrine and devoid of intellectual content. It is established on the needs of the individual, not on any commands of an external God'.[32]

His conclusion is that it had nothing to do with 'the exacting demands of authentic religion'. Norman's argument is as much theological as sociological, yet it is interesting to note how many secular commentators and academics – including many sociologists – share his assumption that 'authentic' religion must be conservative, dogmatic and demanding. More liberal and detraditionalised forms of religion are by the same token viewed as somehow less real. But why should this be the case, and what scholarly grounds are there for making such a judgment? Religion takes many forms, ranging from the strongly differentiated communal types on the one hand to more individualistic forms of inner spirituality on the other, and the judgment that one is more authentic than the others seems more appropriate to the preacher than to the student of religion.

In its own terms, the Religion of the Heart is as religious or, to use vocabulary its adherents might prefer, as spiritual as any other. Diana herself certainly understood it in spiritual terms, and Norman's charge that her humanitarianism was 'secularised' seems far from the mark. There is little trace of atheism in Diana, and no trace of a scientific materialism. Her humanitarianism was spiritual because, as we have seen, its object – the human – had attached to itself the aura of the sacred. Certainly, this spiritual humanism is far from a worked-out metaphysic and certainly, as Norman points out, it has little intellectual content and even less doctrine. Insofar as the Religion of the Heart does have a metaphysical stance, it is alarmingly fluid and imprecise. It can take either a theistic form – in which the ultimate value of the human is inscribed by its Creator – or a non-theistic, New Age, form in which the human is viewed as participating in the divine. Equally, it can combine both forms in the way in which Diana seems to have done, and which inevitably appears confused and contradictory to academic theologians. Yet for those like Diana and her astrologer-advisor Penny Thornton who view religion as a practical rather than an intellectual matter, this is unproblematic. As Thornton commented in 1991, Diana is now 'firmly on her spiritual path. She lives her beliefs. She doesn't pontificate about them. There is no split intellectually. She simply lives these beliefs. She can go into a hospital room and bring light and joy and comfort'.[33] And as one of a number of the angry Christians who responded to Edward Norman's criticisms of Diana in the *Church Times* commented, '"to visit the fatherless and widows in their affliction" is as much part of religion as holding correct doctrines'.[34]

The answer to the question whether the Religion of the Heart is really a religion must therefore be 'yes but' – the 'but' being that it is more individualistic, voluntaristic, detraditionalised, deinstitution-alised and unregulated than the forms of Christianity which very often shape the Western understanding of 'authentic religion'.

The question about the extent to which the Religion of the Heart exerts influence cannot be answered as easily. Because this form of religion has not been clearly labelled and identified in the way that Christianity or even New Age have been, quantitative surveys of religion and values rarely ask the questions which could help elicit information about its significance. In Britain, the best evidence to date is therefore supplied by the response to Diana and to her death in itself. Obviously not everyone who mourned her passing shared her religious ideals. Yet tributes to Diana by journalists, statesmen, and members of the public who were interviewed by the media, or who wrote in books of condolence or left cards suggest that a significant number did.

One very revealing piece of evidence is the number of people who acknowledged Diana's humanitarian contribution. The majority of tributes by public figures and journalists seem to have used this language, and to have used it as an unquestioned and unquestionable discourse of approbation: 'She was a symbol of selfless humanity' (Earl Spencer); 'The world has lost one of its most compassionate humanitarians' (Elton John); 'Princess Diana was the most beautiful symbol of humanity and love for all the world' (Luciano Pavarotti); 'In life, Diana's humanitarian work gave comfort to thousands and a much-needed sense of purpose to herself. In death, her contributions go on and on' (*Newsweek* Commemorative Issue). As supplementary comments make clear, the humanitarianism for which Diana was being celebrated was the warm, emotional, tender-hearted humanitarianism with which she had become associated. As the final quotation at the start of this essay illustrates, the claim was even made that Diana's death had contributed to the spread of a Religion of the Heart: 'The Diana Effect: Charity donations up, Crime down, Little acts of kindness on the increase'. The magazine which carried these headlines on its front cover marshalled the following additional evidence in its story: the Queen drops formalities; people reassess their priorities; we become a nation of flower givers; Oasis donate profits from their Paris concert to AIDS charity. 'The nation', it concluded,

> *'has started to place a greater value on kindness and compassion... We are learning to love each other, just as [Diana] always wanted... Quite simply, we've glimpsed a vision of society where people pull together and show tenderness to one another – and we liked what we saw. Who would have thought that the legacy of our shy, insecure, sensitive princess, would be a vision of Utopia?'*

As some of those who have begun to analyse tributes to Diana have already noticed, language and symbols of the 'heart' were ubiquitous:[35] 'Diana Princess of Wales, gone from our lives but not from our hearts'; 'Dear Diana you will live on in our hearts, our Queen of Hearts. God Bless'; 'Heaven has gained but we are left with broken hearts'; 'You can now rest eternally in our hearts'. Similarly, her 'love', 'kindness' and compassion' are repeatedly celebrated: 'Diana you gave yourself to the world, we will never forget you'; 'Your kindness and love will not be matched by any other'; 'So caring, so loving, so beautiful'; 'Princess of kindness now with your loved one in heaven'; 'So beautiful, so caring, so courageous, an inspiration to us all'. And the belief in the spiritual nature of the human is applied to Diana herself on a regular basis. Many of the tributes address Diana as a being who is still alive, who is looking down on the scene, who dwells in heaven. Some ask her to intercede: 'Good night Princess. Look over us all from above and shine'; 'Princess now a goddess, remembered eternally'. Several rejoice that she is now with Dodi: 'Diana and Dodi be happy together in heaven'. Some speak of her as an angel, or as with the angels where she belongs: 'Diana the gods have taken you as they needed a guardian angel. Love you'; 'Much loved and missed, a beautiful Princess truly an angel now'. Others comment that God has taken her home where she belongs: 'Diana the Heavenly gates were opened, a gentle voice said "come"'; 'A pure English rose lent not given to bud on earth then bloom in heaven'; 'Diana tragic life very tragic death now back in heaven. God bless'; 'Dear Diana you're not dead, God waiting for you around the corner'; 'She loved all./ That's our Di/ she lit the earth now the sky'.[36]

Diana's death and the events which surrounded it thus furnish some important, if imprecise evidence, about the influence of the Religion of the Heart in Britain. Forthcoming studies of reactions to her death outside Britain may offer further information about its influence elsewhere. No such evidence, however, will substitute for serious empirical study of contemporary beliefs, values, and sources of significance. One of the few such studies with a direct bearing on the Religion of the Heart is that by Nancy Ammerman and a team of researchers who surveyed a range of different types of Christian congregation (Protestant and Catholic) across the United States in the 1990s, using both qualitative and quantitative methods.[37] One of Ammerman's most surprising findings was that the majority (51%) of the 1,564 Christians who supplied information about their understanding of the Christian life could be classified not as evangelical (29%), nor as activist (19%), but as belonging to a category which Ammerman labels 'Golden Rule Christians'. Ammerman's description of Golden Rule ('do unto others as you would be done by') Christianity shows it to be identical with what I am here calling Religion of the Heart, but in a more clearly Christian guise than in Diana's version. Golden Rule Christianity is not dogmatic, but is a form of lived religion whose first principle is 'care for relationships, doing good deeds, and looking for opportunities to provide care and comfort for people in need'. It may, Ammerman concludes, 'be the dominant form of religiosity among the middle-class suburban Americans in our study'.[38]

I said at the start of this chapter that the Religion of the Heart was superbly well adapted to late modernity. Evidence like Ammerman's would seem to bear this out. It would take at least another chapter to explain why I make this assertion, but a few broad brush strokes will have to suffice. If one thinks of late modernity in terms of two triumphs – the triumph of the market economy (in an increasingly 'disorganised' form) and the triumph of the democratic polity – then the Religion of Humanity can be seen to legitimate and mesh with both. It fits with the market economy by being fully compatible with the sort of 'spiritual shopping' Paul Heelas describes in the previous chapter, as well as through its endorsement of self-fulfilment and 'pampering' rather than asceticism or self-sacrifice. And it fits with democracy through its hostility towards established authorities of all types and its empowerment of each individual in his or her ordinariness and 'humanity'. Furthermore, one could argue that through its sacralisation of the sphere of intimate and domestic relationships, the Religion of the Heart fits well with the process of social differentiation whereby religion's sphere of activity shrinks from the public and political to the private – though the universal humanitarian outreach of such religiosity must not be forgotten.

One study, one funeral, one princess, and some speculation about religion in late modernity are hardly enough to determine the extent of the influence of the Religion of the Heart. They are, however, suggestive. What they suggest is that in religious matters, as in so much else, Diana acted as a sort of magnifying glass of popular tastes and trends, of commonly held beliefs and widely cherished ideals. The paradox, of course, is that this 'people's religion' should be reflected and popularised by so privileged a being as a princess.

## References

1   *Church Times*, 24 October 1997, p.1.
2   Reported by Rosa Monckton, 'My Friend Diana', in *Diana: A Celebration of Her Life*, *Newsweek* Commemorative Issue. November, 1997, p. 111.
3   The picture appears with caption on the back cover of Anne Sebba's

*Mother Teresa 1910-1997: Beyond the Image*, New York, Doubleday, 1997.

4 Mother Teresa of Calcutta, *A Gift for God. Prayers and Meditations*, San Francisco, Harper Collins, 1996, pp.63-64.

5 Interview with Malcolm Muggeridge, *Something Beautiful for God. Mother Teresa of Calcutta*, San Francisco, Harper and Row, 1986, p. 92.

6 Mother Teresa of Calcutta, *A Gift for God*, p.70.

7 Lady Colin Campbell, *The Real Diana*, New York, St Martin's Press, 1998.

8 Malcolm Muggeridge, *Something Beautiful for God*, p. 15.

9 Ibid. p. 107.

10 Ibid. p. 113

11 Margaret Holder writing in *OK!* magazine, Issue 126, 4 September 1998, pp.79-80. Lady Colin Campbell reports that Diana sometimes accompanied Basil Hume, Cardinal Archbishop of Westminster, on visits to the homeless in his archdiocese, partly because of the influence of Mother Teresa (*The Real Diana*, p.162).

12 Andrew Morton, *Diana. Her True Story in Her Own Words*, London, Michael O'Mara, 1997, p.53; Andrew Morton, *Diana: Her New Life*, London, Michael O'Mara, 1995, p.15. November 1997, p. 111

13 Ernst Troeltsch, *The Social Teaching of the Christian Churches*, 2 vols, London, George Allen and Unwin Ltd., New York; The Macmillan Company, 1931.

14 All quotations from Humphrey Carpenter, *Robert Runcie: The Reluctant Archbishop*, London, Hodder and Stoughton, 1996, pp. 220-225.

15 Ibid. pp. 220-225.

16 Ibid. pp. 222; 224.

17 According to Lady Colin Campbell, this was done in retaliation against Diana who had previously arranged the broadcasting of one of Charles's conversations with Camilla (*The Real Diana*, pp. 175-176).

18 The 'Squidgy' Tape, reprinted in Nigel Dempster and Peter Evans, *Behind Palace Doors. Marriage and Divorce in the House of Windsor*, New York, G.P. Putnam's Sons, 1993, pp. 249-271.

19 Mother Teresa of Calcutta, *A Gift for God*, p.76.

20 See Navin Chawla, *Mother Teresa. The Authorised Biography*, Boston, MA.; Shaftesbury, Dorset; Melbourne, Victoria, Element Books, 1992, pp. 81-82; 178-179.

21 Richard Kay provides a good summary of Diana's contacts with spiritual advisers and therapists towards the end of her life in Richard Kay and Geoffrey Levy, *Diana: The Untold Story*, London, Boxtree and the *Daily Mail*, pp.119-123.

22 Richard Kay and Geoffrey Levy, *Diana: The Untold Story*, p.66.

23 Andrew Morton, *Diana: Her New Life*, p.95.

24 Andrew Morton, *Diana: Her True Story in her Own Words*, p. 72.

25 Ibid. p.70.

26 Cited by Tony Walter, 'Diana, Queen of Hearts. Mourning and Social Solidarity', in John Drane et al., *Death of a Princess. Making Sense of a Nation's Grief*, London, Silver Fish, 1998, p.49

27 Lady Colin Campbell, *The Real Diana*, p.299.

28 Ibid. p. 308

29 Quoted by Tom Masland in, 'A Touch of Humanity', *Newsweek* Commemorative Issue. Diana: A Celebration of Her Life. On sale until 3 November 1997, pp. 62-68.

30 The language of humanitarianism, with its roots in the Enlightenment, is Christian only to the extent that the Enlightenment was itself part of a movement of reform within Christian civilisation. As Stephen Toulmin and others have shown, it was born in part from the desire to achieve peace in a Europe weary of religious wars. Equally, it was tied up with the rise of the new social and cultural élites brought to birth by changing economic and political circumstances. Egalitarian and universalist in its basic thrust, its triumph has been undergirded by the extension of democracy through the intervening centuries. See Stephen Toulmin, *Cosmopolis: The Hidden Agenda of Modernity* Chicago, University of Chicago Press, 1992 and Nathan Sznaider, 'Compassion: the Reconstruction of a Cultural Value', in Cultural Values 2.1 (1998), pp. 117-139.

31 Andrew Morton, *Diana: Her True Story in her Own Words*, pp. 69-70.

32 Edward Norman, 'The Dogma of the Queen of Hearts', *Church Times*, 28 August 1998, p.8.

33 Lady Colin Campbell, *The Real Diana*, p. 135

34 Jeremy Gorling, Letters to the Editor, *Church Times*, 4 September 1998., p.9.

35 See, for example, Ted Harrison, *Diana: Icon and Sacrifice*. Oxford, Lion Publishing, 1998, pp. 167-177.

36 Tributes from: *The People's Pictures. Sun* newspaper's special tribute, 21 August, 1998. pp.20-21.

37 Ammerman's findings are published as *Congregation and Community*. New Brunswick, New Jersey, Rutgers University Press, 1997.

38 Nancy T. Ammerman, 'Golden Rule Christianity. Lived Religion in the American Mainstream' in Donald G. Hall (ed.) Lived Religion in America: *Toward a Theory of Practice*, Princeton, NJ, Princeton University Press, 1997, pp.203' 199.

# 7. Princess Diana as Lady Folly

## Richard Fenn

It is tempting, but too facile, to suggest that Diana was the hallmark of Britain's entry into post-modernity, where fashions, friends, ideas, moods, and personalities engage in a constant game of mix and match. It is tempting, because modern Britain is diverse: a place where people switch channels and employ façades; Diana did embrace diversity, exploit the media, and constantly update her most recent image. If modern Britain enjoys a new publicity for her emotions, it is partly due to Diana's own willingness to go public with her most private sorrows.

To follow these suggestions, however, is to be blind to the presence of the past in all these changes of royal costume. Diana, I will suggest, was acting out a part, one described in detail by Erasmus, that is actually a composite of many roles: court jester, fool, saint, masker, actor, carnival-goer, ecstatic, and lover of souls. More than an unwitting exemplar of these social types, however, Diana also demonstrated the perennial function of play and humour, of compassion and disclosure, of whatever gives heart to a heartless world. From a sociological point of view, that function may simply give temporary relief to an oppressive and unresponsive social order. In concert with certain Christian symbols and memories, beliefs and assumptions, however, the roles of Lady Folly form a cultural template that has long been subversive in pointing to a more genial and humane sort of kingdom and in emphasising the alienating aspects of any social order.

In making this argument, I have no desire to join in the celebration of Diana, but simply to suggest that Lady Folly is the cultural DNA, so to speak, from which the charter, the personality, and also the public function of Diana slowly developed over the years that she suffered and enjoyed her celebrity.

Consider the court jester who makes fun of royalty, perhaps

maliciously, but always with a mixture of candour and deception. Without Lady Folly in the role of the jester, who would remind the court of what makes them human, ordinary, ridiculous, mortal? It is entirely fitting, not only for her character but for the cultural template of Lady Folly herself, that Diana should have been described as not only as 'gentle' but as 'flamboyant': not only 'down to earth' but 'regal', not merely 'foolish' but also 'brave'[1]. Even the so-called wise, who are to be found 'strutting around *like an ape in the king's clothes"...'* are really fools in disguise, and their disguise is pointed out by Lady Folly herself.[2]

> *'Doesn't everyone admit that a king is both rich and powerful? But suppose he possesses none of the gifts of the mind; suppose nothing is ever enough for him: then clearly he is the poorest of the poor..If someone should try to strip away the costumes and the makeup from the actors performing a play on the stage and display them to the spectators in their own natural appearance, wouldn't he ruin the whole play?...the man who played the king only a moment ago would become a pauper.'*[3]

There is nothing very modern about Diana, despite her attempts to remake herself in public through the media. True, in the end Diana did take off the royal makeup and expose the poverty of the Prince and the Royal Family. Nothing is gained, however, by adoring her as a heroine of authentic self-hood, who shaped a public role to her personal satisfaction. Neither is anything gained by complaining that the occasional absence of cosmetics was another façade for self-promotion or that Diana's 'authenticity' allowed her to take satisfaction in exposing the limitations and emotional poverty of the Royal Family. So long as we miss the genuinely antique elements in her performance, we will see Diana only as a feminist victim of patriarchy, a model of independent womanhood, a 'survivor' of life itself, or as an entrepreneur of the wounded self. The images piling up in the press, like the flowers outside Kensington Palace, assume that she was 'one of us' as well as 'one in a million'. If both assessments are right, it is because she bore the *stigmata* of a particular form of cultural heroism: the one whose brush with eternity leaves a taint of divine madness.

The boundary between foolishness and wisdom is drawn far more sharply by moralists and psychologisers than it is in certain parts of the Christian tradition. Certainly it would be a mistake to sneer at Diana's piety. At her funeral this hymn was sung, which sixteen years earlier she had requested be sung at her wedding:

*I vow to thee, my country,*

*all earthly things above,*

*Entire and whole and perfect,*

*the service of my love:*

*The love that asks no question,*

*the love that stands the test,*

*That lays upon the altar*

*the dearest and the best;*

*The love that never falters,*

*the love that pays the price,*

*The love that makes undaunted*

*the final sacrifice.*


*And there's another country,*

*I've heard of long ago,*

*Most dear to them that love her,*

*most great to them that know;*

*We may not count her armies,*

*we may not see her King;*

*Her fortress is a faithful heart,*

*her pride is suffering;*

*And soul by soul and silently*

*her shining bounds increase,*

*And her ways are ways of gentle-*

*ness and all her paths are peace'.*[4]

There is clearly a longing here for another kingdom, in which the wise and powerful of this world are superseded by the reign of the loving and the faithful in a divine realm that lies alongside the realms of this world. Into that heavenly kingdom, however, only the foolish are allowed to enter: not those who are wise according to the lights of this world.

As Erasmus puts it, '...the Christian religion taken all together has a certain affinity with some sort of folly and has little or nothing to do with wisdom.'[5] He notes that the kingdom of fools embodying the wisdom of God lies at the centre not only of the Gospels but of Paul's writing.[6] If Diana was not only young, but, as she appears to have claimed on more than one occasion, also stupid ("Thick as a plank, I am"), she has two of the qualifications for entry into this kingdom; at least Erasmus finds these to be the excuses of the 'mystical psalmist' who pleads his own ignorance and folly, not his malice, as the occasion for receiving divine mercy.[7]

This divine option for the fools of this world, then, is played out in a number of roles, on various stages, but the player is always indebted to this underlying script that subverts what passes for nobility or wisdom, common sense and sound thinking. The role is even harder to identify now than it was in the past, since modern scripts are seldom explicitly Scriptural. Like the movies and music videos that so fascinated the young Diana, modern scripts appear to be recently invented and transparent in their meaning, but are more like fact palimpsests that contain overlays of much earlier writing.

To put it another way: if we are to understand not only Diana but how uncannily familiar she seemed to those who never knew her, we must investigate the possibility that she was perceived as playing an invisible role that is now half-forgotten. The script for the role lies in the neglected parts of Scripture that extol, as Erasmus reminds us, the foolishness of God that is wiser than the wisdom of humanity. No wonder Diana's preferred company resembled those whom Erasmus finds 'more delighted than others with holy and religious matters': by whom he means 'children, old people, women, and retarded persons'.[8]

Even in the sixteenth century, however, we understand from Erasmus that the divine option for the fool was understood least of all by those who prided themselves on their religious offices and their command of Scripture. The wisdom and rationality of those licensed to take themselves seriously obscured then, as now, their own folly

and blinded them to the implicit and hidden knowledge of those
who had been secretly touched by divinity:

> *'And this is Folly's part, which shall not be taken from her*
> *by the transformation of life, but shall be perfected. Those*
> *who have the privilege of experiencing this (and it happens*
> *to very few) undergo something very like madness: they talk*
> *incoherently, not in a human fashion, making sounds*
> *without sense. Then the entire expression of their faces*
> *vacillates repeatedly : now happy, now sad; now crying,*
> *now laughing, now sighing–in short, they are completely*
> *beside themselves.'*[9]

Those who have followed descriptions of Diana in the press will be
reminded of her own volatility in expression, her bouts of depression, her alternating wistfulness and gaiety, and her penchant for
both ecstasy and disappointment.

Thus Erasmus reinvents ancient wisdom in the figure of Lady
Folly, who bears the marks of God's preference for fools and wears
her vestments very lightly. In her role as Lady Folly, as Erasmus has
described her, we find a character whose candour and even
impudence served the purpose of integrating the larger society across
the lines that divided it, and particularly of bringing the monarch
and the people closer together: a noble Lady, but one

> *'...who is willing to run with the herd, to overlook faults*
> *tolerantly or to share them in a friendly spirit. But, they*
> *say, that is exactly what we mean by folly. I will hardly*
> *deny it - as long as they reciprocate by admitting that this is*
> *exactly what it means to perform the play of life.'*[10]

While I am in no position even to guess whether Diana was a secular
sort of saint, Lady Folly has clear precedents in Christian piety; as
with Mary in the well known parable, Erasmus noted in the passage
quoted above that her proximity to the divine is the part that 'shall
not be taken from her'. Indeed, Erasmus argued that Lady Folly can
be understood only if Christians go beyond the formalities of piety
and recover an original passion for transcendence: '...the happiness
which Christians strive for is no more than a certain kind of madness
and folly.'[11]

Indeed, there is even something bulimic about the sort of piety that Erasmus is describing, which seeks total mental control over the body. In the life after death, the soul is 'in its own kingdom now, partly because even in its former life it has purged and refined the body in preparation for such a transformation.'[12] First one is 'purged', and only then does one enter one's own kingdom. In defending itself against excruciating social pressures, the soul is known to retreat into its own mental universe where it can claim a magical sort of sovereignty over the body; there, the psyche seeks to purge itself of whatever it has internalised to its own detriment: food being the outward and visible sign of inward and spiritual malediction.

It is in the fools' search for a private kingdom of their own that we can see and understand some of the aspects of Diana's life that seem most troubling. There was, to begin with, her tendency to drive too fast without a seat belt ,even alone at night through the streets of London. There was, as I have noted, her bulimia, which may have been another effort, as Erasmus would put it, to free a mind 'prevented by the body's grossness from contemplating and enjoying things as they truly are'.[13] There were her attempts to take her own life, as though she sought to free herself once and for all from the burden of the flesh, and also her periodic bouts of depression, when she may well have felt herself weighed down by the physical and social constraints of the royal household: hence her moments of apparent abandon or despair. Furthermore, Diana would occasionally announce her intention to withdraw from the exhausting discipline that she had imposed on herself in visiting the sick and the poor. It is in these moments of withdrawal and self-abandon that we can find that peculiar mixture of self-destructive tendencies and the effort to free what is left of the psyche from the burden of expectation. To free herself from the photographers who ceaselessly trailed her was thus not only a desperate attempt to achieve privacy, but to destroy the image that others had of the princess: images that may well have reminded her too grossly of her body or that required her to live up to impossible expectations. This search for an alternative society or kingdom makes the fool seem vulnerable and precarious, even as the fool sees the taken-for-granted social order itself as resting on the sandiest of foundations.

To preserve a little area of limited autonomy and self-direction, where one can feel oneself vital and alive on one's own terms, some do withdraw into a kingdom of their own: 'soul by soul and silently', as Diana's favourite hymn put it in describing that other kingdom where there is only peace. As Erasmus noted, there is a peculiar affinity between madness and piety in the effort of the mind to find its own kingdom apart and away from the burdens of citizenship in the kingdoms of this world, as '...the mind, being now a little freer from the contagion of the body, begins to exercise its own inborn powers.'[14]

Those who achieve this partial and precarious freedom of the soul sometimes 'have a sort of divine aura about them'.[15] They may also be on a path toward self-destruction. Although the role of Lady Folly therefore relieves the loneliness of social life for many, it nonetheless requires a certain holy madness that sees this life as a mere shadow of the real thing and longs accordingly for immortality. Lady Folly, according to Erasmus is 'the true *dispenser of divine gifts...*'[16] No wonder, then, that Earl Spencer, in his eulogy at Westminster Abbey, not only referred to Diana's 'particular brand of magic' but noted that 'she needed no royal title to continue to generate' that extraordinary grace.

Certainly, the presence of Lady Folly is also dangerous, as well as essential, for any social order. When charisma, grace, breaks through, the world that seemed solid suddenly appears flimsy and not to be taken too seriously. In the hands of a Lady Folly, the noble may seem ludicrous, the taken-for-granted distribution of social honour may resemble a farce, the mute and inglorious may become eloquent, and things as they might be seem more pressing and possible than things as they are. Laughter, as Berger has argued in his most recent work, makes the social world seem precarious indeed.[17] When the real magician appears, all the other magicians suddenly appear phony.

There is also a certain loneliness attached to this role that can be spiritually very dangerous indeed. To be lonely because one goes through motions that mean more to others than to oneself ... or to say words that - like Diana's marriage vows - meant far more to her than to her prince - compounds the weight of social expectation with the realisation that one's soul is not what, to others ,it might seem to be. No one knows this more intensely than the younger members of the Royal Family who are called upon to perform when they are least ready to stand public scrutiny and have not yet acquired the internal personal grace to accompany its outward expression. This is not

merely a dilemma imposed by the requirements of public performance, however; even in the roles of everyday life that everyone
performs, one is kept under critical surveillance without being fully
known. No wonder the toxic compound of duty and loneliness may
be most dangerous for those who remain opaque to others and
themselves.

Such loneliness – the isolation of the self from others with whom
one nevertheless interacts to keep life going – is part of what Erasmus
means by the 'play' of life. Erasmus has Lady Folly saying:

> *'But for God's sake, I wish they would tell me, is there any
> part of life that is not sad, cheerless, dull, insipid, and
> wearisome unless you season it with pleasure, that is, with
> the spice of folly?'[18]*

No wonder Diana '...feasted on romance novels, movie magazines
and music videos'.[19]

Mimicry and joking, for which Diana was renowned, are for
Lady Folly ways '...to dispel the inherent tedium of living'.[20] They
are the antidote to the melancholy, depression, loneliness, and
suicidal tendencies for which also Diana was well known. Jocularity
and giggles, lacerating humour and simple mockery may serve to
alleviate tedium, to fend off social pressures, to defend the psyche
against depression, and even to protect the soul from self-
destructive tendencies. In connection with what Simon Schama
called the 'other England', which is 'rowdy, inventively insolent,
street-smart, and genuinely democratic', Diana as Lady Folly could
make a powerful alliance against the grey and soul-crushing domination not only of the Palace but of Thatcherism.[21] Diana was the
antidote to Margaret Thatcher, as Schama argued, just as surely as
she was toxic to the monarchy.[22]

Lady Folly's gift comes with a reminder that the receiver – like
the gift itself – is here only for the time being. It is not surprising
that Diana found comfort in the presence of those who, sick or
terminally ill, had lost whatever veneer they may have had in the
past and were simply there for the time being. Yet even in this
persistent, however intermittent, devotion to the sick and the
maimed, Diana's devotion was entirely for the time being. She is
reported to have said that she could give love 'for a minute, for a half
an hour, for a day, for a month '.[23] There was something exceedingly

temporal about these gifts: seasonal and evanescent, like the gift of grace itself.

Lady Folly finds enduring contact with being itself only in fleeting moments of extraordinary solitude and private ecstasy that make all the rest of time appear to be merely temporal. However, these brief contacts, like her brief moments with the sick and the poor, had enduring quality. On a card accompanying flowers the Duchess of York, although allegedly estranged from her old friend, referred to Diana, along with other endearments, as her 'soul-mate and partner'. The spiritual partnership endures, even though the relationship was as temporary and as ephemeral as many others in Diana's train.

Some might argue that Lady Folly is a poor cultural model for our understanding of Diana. After all, did not Erasmus say that Folly is tolerant, friendly, the spice of life? But Diana, as we know, was at times a severe embarrassment to the Royal Family, and at other times more like an implacable antagonist in letting the world know about the insufficiencies of the Prince and the Queen and the chilling effect of Palace routine on both the mind and the body. She also brought occasional embarrassment to her political allies, as in her advocacy of the very ban on land mines that was being opposed by the Conservative government. It is the mark of Folly, however, to have 'a certain openminded frankness [and] to take everyone as your equal'.[24] The very egalitarian assumptions that linked Diana to the poor and forgotten also gave her permission to confront the noble or the powerful on their own territory; '...only fools have a license to declare the truth without offence'.[25]

If Diana was an adept at using the media to embarrass the royal household, she had antecedents in the medieval fools, whose freedom allowed them to disenchant sacred mysteries. Of course, the medieval court fool also had a 'precarious' existence, as Berger puts it, being dependent on 'the goodwill of the monarch' and subject to the monarch's 'shifting moods and prejudices'.[26] Thus ,the fool had to be not only witty but 'cunning' and was often malicious, even while being the object of considerable affection.[27] It is no accident that in her life, as in her death, Diana made the royals seem mute and inglorious: the so-called 'waxwork royals'.

Some would argue that courts and regimes are more secure when they have with them a court jester, a fool, a professionalised source of satire: someone, like Diana, herself a 'Lady Folly'. Diana's use of costume to mimic uniform was itself a sign that she was laughing at the royal tendency to enjoy

> '...*the applause of fools, to take pleasure in the cheers of the crowd...Such foolishness as this creates states, it constitutes empires, civil offices, religion, counsels, judgments – in fact, human life is nothing more than an entertainment staged by Folly'.*[28]

As Lady Folly, Diana thus enjoyed her own performances while making the pomp of the Prince look even more foolish. Diana as Lady Folly was thus a double agent, undermining the very plays that she so carefully staged. In the view of the director of Burke's Peerage, the inevitable TV reruns of her life '...will seriously weaken the fabric of the Establishment and could conceivably bring about a republic'.[29]

It is inevitable that Diana, as Lady Folly, should have spoiled the royal party. In the retinue of Lady Folly are a number of attendants: self-love, flattery, rowdiness, luxury, madness, and pleasure, and she claims to have been nursed by 'two most elegant nymphs: Methe (Drunkeness), begotten by Bacchus, and Apaedia (Stupidity)'.[30] It is therefore fitting that Diana should have laid claim to food addiction, to being 'thick', as well as having demonstrated her love of fun, pleasure, and 'ill-judged public romps with her clownish sister-in-law, Sarah Ferguson'.[31]

It is because her gifts and her presence, her relationships and her commitments are at once so ephemeral and enduring that Diana's performance of Lady Folly should have made life bearable for so many.[32] Indeed, Lady Folly provides relief from surveillance and social scrutiny; Erasmus asks,

> '... *how could the joy of friendship possibly last even for a single hour among these "critics who ferret out every fault" if it were not for...."folly" or "an easy-going temperament"'*?[33]

Lady Folly thus serves a crucial social function to 'join together the whole framework of society and make the wheels of life run smoothly'.[34] Without Lady Folly's ministrations not only marriages and friendships, but every relationship of unequal status and authority would turn sour, and 'the people would no longer tolerate their prince'.[35]

It is not an accident, then, that her brother, Earl Spencer, should speak of her in his eulogy as 'someone with a natural nobility who was classless': an apt description of the person Diana became in her many roles that brought her directly in touch with a wide variety of victims and sufferers. More to the point, that phrase captures just what Erasmus had in mind in portraying Lady Folly as the one whose natural grace gives temporary solace and occasional joy to any society in which social distinctions prove not only invidious but destructive. Even the monarchy briefly became once again imaginable as the cultural centre of an increasingly diverse society. No wonder that one of the mourners placed this card among the flowers before Kensington Palace:

> *'Dear Diana Thank you for treating us like human beings -
> not criminals. You were one in a million. From David
> Hayes and all the lads in H.M.Prison, Dartmoor.'*

It is therefore no surprise that in the days between Diana's death and her funeral, the streets outside Kensington palace were lined with 'all sorts and conditions'. There was something truly catholic in the taste of the people for Diana, and in Diana's taste for the people.

Lady Folly is the one who embodies the people and makes them real to the world of priests and kings. The people were embodying her, making her - and themselves - unforgettably visible to monarchy. They were not to be ignored or forgotten in her death, just as she made them visible in her life. In losing Diana, the British monarchy lost someone who, more than any other in recent memory, had played the role of the fool - the jester - as intermediary between people and king. The loss of that intermediary moved Tony Blair to use the phrase 'The People's Princess' and to counsel the Royal Family on their public expression of grief.

It is therefore no accident that, for a time, the monarchy seemed even more precarious after Diana's death than it did while she was making a mockery of it in her lifetime. Diana, as Lady Folly, had been a source of crucial information about the environment: the people's anger, needs, troubles, passions, etc. It may or may not be demonstrable that, after the French court finally rid itself of its jesters, the monarchy became more vulnerable to revolution. It is nonetheless dangerous to part with Lady Folly, for the same reasons that it is dangerous for any social system to lose its capacity for self-criticism, its awareness of dissent and discontent, and its capacity to imagine another way of doing things.

The presence of folly should render regimes more open to suggestion, more self-critical, and therefore less likely to be surprised by the strength of popular passions. However, it would be a mistake to underestimate the foolishness of the state in suppressing this alternative form of wisdom. That mistake is as old as Folly herself. The authors of the recently published study of *The Religions of Rome* wisely point out the reasons for the official attacks on the cult of Isis during the first century B.C.:

> *'The cult of Isis, with its independent priesthood and its devotion to a personal and caring deity could represent (like the Bacchic cult) a potentially dangerous alternative society, out of the control of the traditional political elite.*[36]

The notion that a 'personal and caring deity' could be a source of subversion is especially appropriate to any assessment of Diana as Lady Folly; she was the one whose devotion to the weak and ignored amounted to a standing rebuke of the existing social order: a condemnation not only of its Thatcherite cruelties and of the monarchy, but of an entire system.

Lady Folly is a cultural template that opens each society to what is alien within its own borders. No doubt that template owes much to the Christian tradition that subverts the existing order and presents a vision of a world in which it does not hurt to be kind. As Lady Folly, Diana could fulfill her vision, so well expressed in her favourite hymn, of 'another country' whose ways are gentle and peaceful.

However, the belief in another country, radically more 'personal and caring' than this one, often makes one feel like a stranger and even act strangely. That is partly because the notion of 'another country' in whose citizenship true joys can be found, is fundamental to the religious subversion of normalcy. In that country, for instance, there is quite another version of suffering: one which ends the warfare between pride and suffering. The proud are made to suffer, and the suffering keep their pride. Diana's residence in exile would have been intended as a perpetual reminder that there is another country in which love prevails over reasons of state and over administrated cruelty.

Strangeness is normal in that other country to which Diana aspired. At least, it is in keeping with Lady Folly's role that Diana should have been rumoured to have planned to leave England in order to take up her residence in another country.

If true, this would not have been simply because Diana's enthusiasm for another sort of society had made her a very cosmopolitan princess or because she died as she was speeding away in the company of an Arab suitor. As Lady Folly herself puts it, 'among the pleasures I offer, one of the most refined is to value most highly what is most foreign.'[37]

If there is any tendency to turn Diana into the object of a cult, to canonise her, or even to report 'sightings' of her, Lady Folly herself would not be pleased. After all, as Erasmus put it,

> '...no one sacrifices to Folly, they say, and no one has built a temple dedicated to her.'[38] Indeed, I myself, as I said, find this ingratitude somewhat surprising. Still, I am good-natured enough to take this also in good part, though I couldn't really want such things anyway... Unless, perhaps, I should envy Diana because human blood is sacrificed in her honour.'[38]

## References

1   Barbara Kantrowitz, Daniel Pedersen and Stryker McGuire, 'The Day England Cried' in *Newsweek* 15 September 1997, p.30.
2   Desiderius Erasmus, *The Praise of Folly*, New Haven and London, Yale University Press, 1979. p. 13.
3   Ibid. p. 43.
4   Quoted in Howard Chua-Eoan, 'In Living memory" *Time* 15 September 1997, p.75.
5   Erasmus, *The Praise of Folly*, p. 132.
6   Ibid.
7   Ibid. p. 131.
8   Ibid. p. 132.
9   Ibid p. 137.
10  Ibid. p. 44.
11  Ibid. p. 132.
12  I bid. p. 135.
13  Ibid. p. 133.
14  Ibid.
15  Ibid.
16  Ibid. p. 13.

17  Peter Berger, *Redeeming Laughter, The Comic Dimension of Human Experience*, New York, Berlin, Walter de Gruyter.
18  Erasmus, *The Praise of Folly*, p. 19.
19  Alessandra Stanley. 'A Fairy-Tale Hamlet with a Diamond Tiara', in *The New York Times*, 7 September 1997, Section 4, p. 1.
20  Erasmus, *The Praise of Folly*, p. 30.
21  Simon Schama, in 'The Problem Princess' *The New Yorker*, 15 September 1997, p. 64.
22  Ibid. p. 64.
23  Howard Chua-Eoan, 'In Living Memory', *Time* 15 September 1997, p.74.
24  Erasmus, *The Praise of Folly*, p. 122.
25  Ibid. p. 123.
26  Peter Berger, *Redeeming Laughter*, p. 75.
27  Ibid.
28  Erasmus, *The Praise of Folly*, p. 41.
29  Harold Brooks-Baker, 'Why Charles Should Go' in *Newsweek* 15 September 1997, p. 57.
30  Erasmus, *The Praise of Folly*, p. 17.
31  Alessandra Stanley, 'A Fairy-Tale Hamlet with a Diamond Tiara' in *The New York Times*, 7 September 1997, Section 4 p. 5.
32  'In short, without me [Lady Folly] no companionship among friends, no blending of lives in marriage can be either pleasant or stable. *The people would no longer tolerate their prince, nor the master his servant...nor the wife her husband....*if in their relations with one another they did not sometimes err, sometimes flatter, sometimes wisely overlook things, sometimes soothe themselves with the sweet salve of folly.' Erasmus, *The Praise of Folly*, pp. 33-34.
33  Erasmus, *The Praise of Folly*, p. 32.
34  Ibid. p.33
35  Ibid.
36  Mary Beard, John North, Simon Price, *Religions of Rome, Volume 1. A History*. Cambridge, Cambridge University Press, 1998. p. 161.
37  Erasmus, *The Praise of Folly*, p. 14.
38  Ibid. p. 74-75.

# 8. Di and Dodi Die

## Simon Critchley

It is now two weeks later, 15 September 1997, and I am travelling on the U-Bahn in Frankfurt, which is home for this year. Looking up from my newspaper across the crowded carriage, I see a young black woman, about 25 years old. With great deliberateness, she takes a single photocopied sheet of paper out of her bag and begins to read. I return to my newspaper: a fascinating discussion of the failing proposals for tax reform in the Bundestag. Looking up again a minute later, I notice that she is crying, tears are streaming down her face and she is quietly sobbing. She has let the photocopied sheet rest on her knees. I crane my neck to try and read the text. It is a German translation of Elton John's 'Candle in the Wind 97', which appeared in the wonderfully shameful *Bild*, the German equivalent to *The Sun*. The sheet of paper is slightly crumpled and tatty at the edges: it is clearly not the first time she has read it. We both get out at the same U-Bahn station and I quickly lose sight of her in the crowd. Strange, I think.

\* \* \*

I was myself strangely moved by Diana's death. Like so many others. And I take no pride in admitting this. It came as something of a surprise. As a right-thinking leftist, I have always been resolutely anti-monarchist, desiring nothing more than Britain might become a republic, like other normal countries. After a couple of drinks, I have even been known to quote from memory whole passages from Tom Paine's *Rights of Man* and hum verses from Blake's "Jerusalem".

At the beginning, I was not particularly fond of Diana. However, I swapped my early view that she was simply a typically brain-dead member of the ruling class, whose inviolate womb could be of service to the future of the House of Windsor, for a later view that she was rather cunning, clever even. I was reluctantly impressed by her careful stage-management and manipulation of the British press. As became clear in her extended TV interview on the BBC's *Panorama* in 1995, which captivated and even shocked me, this was someone who seemed to have a powerfully intuitive sense of how to outflank the members and defenders of the House of Windsor. She was trouble. And on the principle that my enemy's enemy is my friend, I began to like her. In the last couple of years, I followed her adventures much more closely and was absolutely delighted when she met and clearly fell in love with Dodi Al Fayed. As will be clear to anyone who remembers the ugly, shameful and racist campaign against the Al Fayed brothers' takeover of Harrods in London, led by Tiny Rowland, head of Lonrho and former owner of *The Observer*, Diana's affair with Dodi was potential political dynamite and a palpable threat to the British Establishment. Her final interview with *Le Monde*, published just a week or so before her death, seemed to confirm her nascent political role as strenuously as she denied it. Her criticism of ministers of the former Conservative government and her support for the Labour party policy on the issue of landmines (as I write, news has just come through from Oslo that the Nobel Peace Prize has been awarded to Jody Williams and the campaign against land mines) was a new, if awkward, departure for her. Diana's life had been gathering a powerful and dangerous momentum, and her untimely death now appears like a destiny.

There is much to say about Diana's death, which is possibly the biggest single *event* in world history, if we define an event as something contemporary which living human beings share, whether immediately or through the various media. However, all I want to explore here, briefly, is why it is that this death should be so *moving*, not only for me, but for the stranger on the U-Bahn in Frankfurt, and for so many others. Obviously, what is at issue here is the question of feeling, emotion or affect and the seemingly overwhelming requirement on the part of countless millions of people, to find a *meaning* for this affect.

\* \* \*

Isn't the trauma and drama of Diana's death the *risk of the potential meaninglessness of pain?* What I mean can be expressed in terms of the plucky Earl Spencer's words from his unprecedentedly critical eulogy. He said that it was Diana's own experience of pain that allowed her to be moved by, and be compassionate towards, other people. It was her own sense of agony and deep personal worthlessness that allowed her to reach out to others that she found in a similar situation. And this was also obviously why she was so loved, because people sensed her deep vulnerability and identified their pain, their hurt, and their grief with hers. In that sense, she was a representation or symbol of the fact of pain, and provided a meaning to people's basic sense of hurt. Here was a stylish, compassionate woman who had clearly been wronged, and her admirers could identify their own wrongs with hers and render them meaningful. Her death, then, is the trauma of the disappearance of this symbol, of this means of identification, where meaning collapses, and the subject is left with the *noesis* of subjective affect without the *noema* of an intentional object.

And this is what is so extraordinary about what happened after Diana's death, reaching a climax with her funeral. Faced with the disappearance of what seemed to symbolise people's personal experience of pain and guarantee some kind of meaning, one was overwhelmed with the sheer *demand* for meaning – 'This has to mean something, otherwise nothing means anything'. What was most striking in the hours and days after her death was that there was very little to say, but an overwhelming desire to say *something*. What happened at her funeral and in the days before was that this demand for meaning was articulated *publicly*. Faced with the potential meaninglessness of pain, people (and not simply the media) made a public meaning out of this possibly meaningless and tragic death. It is an impressive sight to watch infinitely long lines of ordinary people waiting *quietly* for hours to sign the books of condolence, or to watch untold thousands of inhabitants of North London *quietly* placing flowers on the funeral hearse. This had not happened before. How did everyone know what to do?

So, all it seems to take in order to shore up the loss of meaning is to stand together quietly with your fellow human beings. The fact of one's own sense of pain, of hurt and grief, is assuaged by forms of public display. Of course, this is not exactly news. It is why we have funerals. However, what is intriguing to me in Diana's death is that the need for a symbolisation that approximates to the fact of grief. and which requires a public form of display, also seems to articulate a demand for *justice*. I remember watching BBC Breakfast TV two days before the funeral, when people were beginning to gather on The Mall so that they could better pay their respects to the funeral *cortège*. Most of them had just awoken from a first night sleeping outside on the pavement, and they were being interviewed by a suitably bouncy and hopeless young reporter who clearly hadn't met people like this during her years reading Eng. Lit. at Oxford. But despite her crass insensitivity – 'Well, why are *you* here?' – what was so impressive was the patience, quietness and fumbled yet firm articulacy of the people being interviewed: 'Well, it's just wrong isn't it? And we are here because it's what Diana would have wanted'. In these words, and so many others spoken in the days and weeks after Diana's funeral, is a barely articulated demand for justice, that something is wrong and something ought to be done to right this wrong.

As has been pointed out, Diana's death is a tragedy in the Greek sense. It is the heroic sacrifice of a flawed and wronged human being, with whom the spectators in the global media theatre can identify as a universal figure. And in our mourning for this unjust death at the hands of what looks like power (the media, the House of Windsor), there seems to be a cleansing, a purgation or purification, some sort of *catharsis*. Diana's death – which is truly *death by publicity*, with the paparazzi in the role of Aeschylus' Furies – demands another public form of symbolisation and meaning-conferral, a display which is some response to the injustice of her death and an aspiration to justice, to right this wrong. One thinks of the end of *The Oresteia*, where the *polis* is cleansed and there is the torchlight descent of the *cortège* into Athens, to install justice into the public realm.

Picking up the question of Diana as a universal tragic heroine, what is so curious about this event, for someone from Britain, is its extraordinary significance at the international level. I was attending a political science conference in Washington DC and enjoying a late dinner with some American colleagues when the news of Diana's death came through. Our Brazilian waiter broke the news, and I stupidly asked him to repeat what he said three times because I didn't believe it. I was stunned, and then utterly taken aback by the American reaction to Diana's death. I remember sitting until 4.00 a.m. in the lobby at the Sheraton watching CNN and trying to fit the pieces of the story together, given the scant information available. All around me American academics, respectable political scientists, were openly weeping. Very strange.

However, the American interest in Diana is perhaps not so surprising, as the USA seems to desire a monarchy more than anyone else; some interstitial space of mythical authority that is partially filled by the cult of celebrity and the Hollywood aristocracy (Tom Cruise was one of the first people CNN got to comment on Diana's death). But why, to return to my opening anecdote, should a young woman in Frankfurt weep over the words of Elton John?

In a word, it is because of *compassion*. What I mean is that Diana became some sort of universal lightning rod for people's sense of hurt, wrong and pain. People identified their pain with hers, and then reflected her obvious compassion with their own sense of compassion. What seemed to be articulated in the days after Diana's death, and particularly at her funeral, was something like *the primacy of compassion*, and the overwhelming demand for it to be publicly displayed as collective grief. And such compassion is not something apolitical, but rather an experience that might be said to contain within it the demand for political justice, for wrongs to be put right, for hurt to be heard, for personal pain to be assuaged by becoming public.

Doubtless, I am going too far, and one might rightly object that this demand for justice is for the most part pretty reactionary, particularly in a British context, where a fairly distasteful nationalism is at work, exemplified in the bewilderingly mixed metaphors of Elton John's 'Goodbye, England's rose'. Of course, one might also say, after Hannah Arendt, that if Diana's death reveals the primacy of compassion or the care principle, then this is politically corrosive and not productive. And maybe Diana's death should be interpreted more pessimistically, in terms of the endless Lacanian mirror-plays of ideology and subjection *à la* Slavoj Zizek. Of course, the easiest intellectual response to Diana's death is cynicism, but perhaps this is simply a form of self-protection that misses what is interesting in this event.

\*   \*   \*

Let me conclude with some remarks on pain as a political factor. This was most immediately and amusingly evident in the way people laying flowers outside the numerous impromptu shrines started attacking journalists and kicking over camera equipment - 'Well, it's you that killed her.!' But Diana's death also raises interesting questions about the nature and possible crisis of constitutional monarchy.

'You cannot trust the people to be rational' - such is arguably the basic premise of constitutional monarchy in Great Britain, as Montesquieu realised. Given that human beings are not fully rational, but are subject to irrational emotions and feelings, the modern state has to be constructed in the light of this fact. Hence, the most rational form of government, republicanism, is too risky and too insecure because of the unenlightened state of the unwashed majority of the population. Therefore, the political form of society has to reflect this relative lack of enlightenment in the populace and maintain forms of political identification that are essentially leftovers from pre-Enlightenment societies. Hence the need for a monarch, to provide that emotional or affective object of identification that allows the people to *feel* as if they belong, to be loyal to the nation whilst their paid representatives can get on with the rational business of government. The monarch is the *mythical* basis of political authority in constitutional monarchy, even though the King or Queen has only symbolic power (but one should not underestimate the power of symbolism with the qualification 'only') and the sovereign is paradoxically subject to the sovereignty of Parliament.

This generation of mythic affect is something that the House of Windsor achieved to a remarkable extent, hand in glove with the rabidly nationalistic tabloid press, employing the myth of the monarch and the idea of the Royal Family as a symbolic glue to keep the state intact and maintain popular national feeling. Such affect reached a crescendo with the Queen's Silver Jubilee in 1977, and the royal marriages of the following years: Charles to Diana, Andrew to Sarah Ferguson. The conjuncture of these events with the collapse of the British economy, massive unemployment, violent social unrest, the rise of the New Right, and the hegemony of Thatcherism should be kept firmly in mind. As should the utter cynicism of the Falklands War in 1982, with Prince Andrew in the role of hero as helicopter pilot, and systematic dismantling of the power of organised labour, typified in the barbarity of the 1984-5 miners' strike.

Now, what Diana's death has revealed, in a most surprising and unprecedented way, is how pathologically dysfunctional this form of government has become. Why? Because, as became clear very quickly in the days following the crash in Paris that all this national *feeling* was no longer being directed to the monarch - 'Speak to us, Ma'am', ran the headline in *The Sun* two days before the funeral - and certainly not to the hopeful pretender Charles III, but rather to the dead Diana. What is so odd here is that the national *Volksgefühl* at the basis of the

British state was being directed towards this victim of the state who had been alienated and scorned by the House of Windsor. The most oft-heard complaint in the days following Diana's death was that the Queen, Prince Charles and all the rest, seemed to show no emotion, they did not appear to be moved by events at all. The Princes William and Harry, at Balmoral with their relatives, and being brought up to respect tradition and do their duty, were seen to be treated *heartlessly*. They were awoken in the early hours of 31 August be told of their mother's death, and then were expected to attend church with the rest of the family in the usual way. It is this mood that was caught so well by Earl Spencer when he spoke – and it was almost treason – of the obligation incumbent on the Princes' *blood* family to let their 'hearts sing out'. The irrational emotionality at the basis of the political authority of the Royal Family was displaced by Diana's death and was suddenly directed against the House of Windsor.

And one must recall that the Windsors – or Saxe-Coburgs – are a very strange bunch: emotionally introverted and detached, their only redeeming characteristic is a hollow, irony-ridden, humour flapping at the edges of an inflexible sense of duty and tradition. What's more, they have been revealed to be utterly out of step with the people. The problem is that the more that someone like Charles now attempts to articulate his sorrow and regret, the less people believe him and the more they doubt his integrity. His succession to the throne is now extremely doubtful. One image repeatedly comes to mind in this respect: as one in a series of unprecedented moves, the entire House of Windsor, all 43 of them present, came to the gates of Buckingham Palace, to pay their respects to the funeral *cortège* as it passed on its way to Westminster Abbey. They were nonchalantly chatting amongst themselves in the way they always do, and were dressed as badly as ever. As the *cortège* passed, they fell silent and bowed their heads. What struck me – and what I keep recalling now – was how completely *helpless* they looked, how utterly out of step they were with the general mood.

So, the event of Diana's death has revealed a crisis at the core of constitutional monarchy in Great Britain. But the consequence of this crisis is not at all clear. Now that the people of England have spoken, will they – and this is something that Christopher Hitchens charmingly suggested, recalling the rhetoric of eighteenth century English republicanism – oust these emotionally inert German imports, these Hanoverian Rats, and move into the rational daylight of a new republic? Will the New Jerusalem be built in England's green and pleasant land (Elton John unwittingly alludes to William Blake)? But however much the ghost of Tom Paine might rattle its chains, and however devoutly one may wish for a Republic of England, in a new confederation with the Republics of Scotland and Wales, and a quite new settlement of the problems English colonialism caused in Ireland, I think this is doubtful. Especially when the man in control is the ever-smiling Tony Blair, who has shown a sureness of political intuition equalled only by the late Princess of Wales (even if he lacks her dress sense). But one can always hope. Revolutions often happen in the strangest ways. After all, it's a free country.

Frankfurt am Main,
14 October 1997

\* \* \*

*Postscript:* Reading this text a year later, I feel rather embarrassed at certain of the rather hopeful views expressed, doubtless caused both by the euphoria of the moment, a certain geographical dislocation on my part caused by living in Germany, and the way the floral revolution followed hard on the 'things can only get better' *Volksgefühl* of Blair's election victory. I don't know what exactly popped the bubble of my enthusiasm, but the words 'Thanks' that appeared on the lid of my tub of Flora Margarine in the late Spring shocked even me. And let's face it, the sight of Chris de Burgh and a portly, out-of-tune Simon Le Bon and Duran Duran at the Diana Commemorative Concert at Althorp certainly didn't help matters. The repeated requests for TV and radio interviews that followed the misquotation of the above text in the *Sunday Times* in March 1998 were a small object lesson of the sort of savagely trivial feeding frenzy on which much of the international media subsists. But to put matters right would require another text, and for that I have neither the inclination nor the inspiration.

Instead of this, let me express my current views on Diana with a joke that I heard on the occasion of the first anniversary of her death. It goes as follows: 'Did you see me on TV at Diana's funeral? I was the one who started the Mexican Wave'. Now, this joke gets funnier the more one thinks about it. One imagines a vast Mexican Wave following the gun carriage through London and down The Mall all the way to the gates of Buckingham Palace. Of course, to be in step with the much-vaunted mood of the nation, the 43 members of the House of Windsor would have to join in with the Mexican Wave, perhaps forming an orderly line with Liz & Cie bowing low and emitting a deep but slightly joyful groan before the Wave wended its way to the gates of Westminster Abbey. In my fancy, I see that Wave sweeping up Finchley Road, all the way to the M 1 and beyond. Who knows, perhaps they are waving still.

Earl's Colne,
22 October 1998.

A version of this chapter first appeared in Theory and Event, Vol. 1, No. 4, 1997.

# 9. The Spatial Diana: The Creation of Mourning Spaces for Diana, Princess of Wales

## Alvin Cohan

In this essay, I wish to speculate about what I have come to think of as the Spatial Diana, the physical places Diana occupied in the weeks following her death. The spatial Diana takes two forms. The first, and the less significant, is connected with the forms of communication that brought news of the death of Diana, Princess of Wales, to people throughout the world, but especially in the United Kingdom. The work of the media in creating a particular picture, or image, of how people feel about her death, which may or may not be grounded in most people's reality, leads to the second aspect of the spatial Diana. This refers to where people chose to mourn and how their actions departed from traditional modes of grieving and/or mourning in British society. Much of what follows is based upon observation of that extraordinary week beginning with the rather ordinary late summer Sunday morning the news of her death transformed. In almost all ways ,this essay is by necessity anecdotal, a form of analysis that, as a behaviourally-trained political scientist I frankly dislike, and with which I feel uncomfortable. But the impressions I formed from what I observed that week and since were so strong that they have led me to try to make some sense of what happened and what it may suggest about contemporary Britain.

This I do as a social scientist with no grounding whatsoever in the sociology of death, a subject area which seems to me to be somewhat lacking in explanations for the collective grief much of the press told us had occurred when news of Diana's death was disseminated. I shall argue that much of the grieving which in Britain has traditionally been understood as a private act, became public as spaces were created for what turned out to be very public mourning. It is my further contention that grief as a private activity was probably substantially less significant than the public displays of sadness. Indeed, what I shall argue is that what Diana's death may have involved was mourning without grief, largely public display with little private feeling. This may be contrasted with the assassination of John F. Kennedy in 1963, when grief and mourning were so obvious in the United States.

To begin, my interest grew out of having moved to London in mid-July 1997. The area of London in which I settled is euphemistically referred to as Highgate Borders (N19 instead of N6). Knowing this is important to the reader in locating mourning spaces later. In fact, Highgate Village is a six-minute walk away from my flat and four minutes to my flat from the Village, given the incline and decline of Highgate Hill. In the month and a half from the time my partner and I moved to that area until Diana's death, I became marginally aware of the fuss which was being made over the budding 'romance' between Diana and Dodi Al-Fayed. This awareness was gained largely from purchasing my regular newspaper, *The Guardian*, at a newsagent where the tabloid headlines were difficult to avoid.

Part of this interest was also rooted in my admiration of the changes the Al-Fayeds had brought about in Harrods as well as the ongoing battle Mohamed Al-Fayed was fighting to acquire British citizenship. At about the same time he was engaged in that fight, I had become a citizen with no trouble at all under the same Home Secretary, Michael Howard. Given my view that economically, Mr Al-Fayed has contributed substantially more to the wellbeing of Britain than my meagre efforts as a university teacher, albeit a dedicated one, his failure to obtain citizenship, something he clearly values, has interested me greatly; this is particularly so in the light of my interest in civil rights and liberties. The pictures of Diana and Dodi filling the newspapers and the subsequent television news programmes seemed surreal to me at best, partly because it appeared so unlikely a match and partly because what they were doing was so profoundly uninteresting. At worst, it struck me that the press was engaged in a mindless intrusion into people's private lives.

On the morning of the accident in Paris, I rose, as I always do, quite early and at 6:30 am dragged a less than willing dog on her morning walk, after which we stopped at our local newsagent located at the entrance to Archway tube station. When I asked for my normal Sunday newspaper, *The Observer*, the newsagent, an Indian, told me no newspapers had arrived. He was completely mystified by it, and surmised that the delivery van may have broken down. I raise the point that he was of Indian origin only because he was listening to the radio tuned to a local station playing Indian music. Had that station announced the death of Diana, I am certain the newsagent would have told me of the occurrence. Indeed, his lack of any understanding as to why the newspapers had not yet arrived suggests he did not know of her death. Several other people were waiting for early morning buses and they, too, were irritated by the absence of their regular newspapers.

I arrived back at the flat just after 7:00 am and was greeted by my partner who would normally have been asleep at that time on a Sunday morning. He was awake because my sister, who lives in Atlanta, Georgia, had just rung. My immediate thought was of an accident or death in my family – it would have been just before 2:00am in Atlanta when my sister rang. I was told no one in the family had died; instead, Ellen had been watching a late night television programme when the news broke of the automobile accident in Paris. She continued to watch television as more news broke finally, ending with the announcement of Diana's death. Ellen then rang us, knowing I am always an early riser. We turned on the television to watch disbelievingly the stories that were filtering through, the beginning of what was to become saturation coverage.

The social scientist part of me was fascinated by the way we obtained the news. An event in Paris, occurring at a time most people in Europe would have been asleep, was transmitted to the United States where people were coming to the end of the evening, and that news was then transmitted back to Europe where the event had actually occurred. All this took place potentially in seconds, the weak link being whether people were actually tuned into the radio or television, in other words, the receiver. Indeed, I was reminded first of the assassination of Robert, not John, Kennedy, following his victory in the California presidential primary in June, 1968. I was in Athens, Georgia, at the time and had been watching with great interest the results of that election coming through. I turned off the television directly after Kennedy's victory statement and went to bed. When I turned on the morning news some five hours later, I was stunned to learn he had been shot minutes after his statement. In contrast, Martin Luther King's murder took place the same year during prime time television viewing. In fact, it coincided with most of the main news programmes, the result being that it was common knowledge early enough for rioting and violence to break out in predominantly black areas of cities throughout the United States. The spatial context was vital in terms of both place and time for what followed immediately after news of his death and the way it had happened became known.

When one considers that at the time of the assassination of President Lincoln in 1865 it would have taken at least a week for information about the President's death to reach Europe, one is reminded of how the flow of communications has altered our lives. Once telegraph and telephones became available, news could be transmitted almost instantaneously, being held up only by those who worked at the point of receipt of the information. With the development of radio and television, any news could be brought directly into an individual's home. The restrictions on news would be based only on what was transmitted. In the Vietnam war, news agencies sent out what they wished, The visual images often ran counter to the message the United States government wanted to send. During the Tet Offensive in 1968, when the government was assuring citizens of the victory over the Viet Cong, those same citizens were watching people who worked in the United States embassy compound in Saigon, ostensibly the safest place in Vietnam, dodging bullets. That image told a far different story than that of the government.

With lessons learned from that era, governments began managing the flow of information as seen in the Falklands War (1982) and later in the Gulf War (1991). But given the nature of the information flows now combined with changes in the nature of journalism, particularly television news, had those wars gone disastrously wrong for Britain in the former case or the Alliance in the latter, the information would have reached the public eventually. Indeed, during the Gulf war, even the journalistic activity, which I would define as the filtering process through which news stories reach the public, was suspended. Instead, the war 'experience' was brought directly to those members of the public who had access to CNN. The broadcasters simply turned their cameras onto the streets of Jerusalem nearest the studios after the first Scud missiles from Iraq had been fired into Israel. Viewers sat for several hours – I was one of them– waiting for something to happen. Local American stations deserted their normal suppliers of national news and also joined the CNN coverage. Alas, for the news media, but luckily for Israeli citizens, except for some lorries driven by, nothing did happen.

In 1989, viewers watched the Romanian revolution, and the collapse of the Communist regime begin, with the rally which was held in an attempt to bolster the Ceausescu government. Previously, views of revolutions had been retrospective, seen through the eyes of film makers and writers reconstructing events. The 'real thing', seen as it happened, was, perhaps, far less heroic in terms of presentation than reconstruction. But the point should be clear that with the potential of instant transmission of news and the spread of information technology, such that any home with the money to spend can tap into a mind-boggling array of information, governments may have reached the point at which they can scarcely control what news populations receive. Indeed, the only brake on it is that the amount of information may be too much for the average citizen to handle.

Without judging the rightness of what happened in the aftermath of the car crash in Paris, it seems almost miraculous in terms of good taste that the pictures we know were taken of the dying Diana and dead Dodi were not flashed around the world. It has been reported that British newspapers turned down offers to buy such pictures. Perhaps the French police headed off early transmission with the arrest of the paparazzi at the scene, but there is no doubt such pictures could have been in the homes of all available viewers before the police intervened. My sister's receipt of the information which she then transmitted to me, could well have been accompanied by the most ghastly of images.

But in terms of information, the spatial possibilities are becoming almost universal. Control of the information spaces must certainly be moving out of government hands and into the hands of broadcasters, and now anyone with transmission access to a telephone point. Diana's death demonstrates this point admirably.

One other point flows from news transmission and our spatial Diana. The speculation about some sort of conspiracy is both fuelled and facilitated by instant communication. Although such speculation has been around as long as notions of conspiracies were first emerging – and both Kennedy assassinations and the murder of Martin Luther King, particularly the first, are testimony. Conspiracy theories, it seems to me, are largely a reflection of the incomprehensible nature of any famous person's death by anything other than what could be seen as natural causes, whether it is the two Kennedys, Marilyn Monroe or Diana. John Kennedy's death at the hands of a 'loser' like Lee Harvey Oswald seems too banal to have occurred in the way the police investigators or Warren Commission described. Perhaps because such deaths are so important in terms of the enormity of their impact, we feel the need to understand them in more dramatic or 'meaningful' terms. The trials and subsequent executions or imprisonment of people implicated in the assassination of President Lincoln bear witness to the ways in which those representing the public may respond when pressed. The responses to bombings and other such events in Britain, and the very public trials ,which resulted in convictions, since overturned as being unsafe, illustrate how easily over-reactions are translated into injustices applied to those thought to be responsible, or, as in the case of the Lincoln killing, those who might have some connection to those responsible.

I raise this point only to distinguish the death of Diana from the others who might be placed firmly in the category of political assassinations. Even looking at Diana's activities with such issues as AIDS and the landmines campaign, she was essentially a non-political figure. Further, being divorced, she no longer had any official status in terms of her relationship to the Royal Family save her position as the mother of a future king. Why, then, was there such a reaction to her death? We have certainly constructed a picture of the mood following her death which most people and analysts have come to accept as what was felt by the nation. Is the construction of a mood of national grief accurate?

My recollection of the Diana Week following the crash is rather different from many of the analyses and accounts of those seven days. Once again, I must rely upon my own memory. But in doing so, I wish to speculate about the reasons for the reactions to Diana's death and the form those reactions took. In this context, I wish to consider some of the terms related to death, and reactions to it and then examine the space in which the public reacted in Diana's case. Once again, I need to refer to personal recollection and experience in London in order to demonstrate the importance of the spatial Diana.

From the time Diana died in the early hours of 31 August until early in the morning of 6 September, the day of her funeral, I was in

London. Because we were relatively new in London, I needed to do a number of chores. I went about this routine which involved forays into central London including Oxford Street, one trip across London to have keys cut in Paddington, shopping in Islington, Hampstead, Camden and Swiss Cottage. I took walks on Hampstead Heath and Waterlow Park, made a couple of trips to the National Film Theatre and had evenings out which took me to Soho, the South Bank and Piccadilly. Most of these places showed evidence of Diana's death , with pictures in shop windows and other displays in building entrances. I went nowhere near Buckingham Palace, Kensington Palace or St. James's Palace, the places where I knew large numbers of people were gathering to bring flowers and be with others. Nor did I go anywhere near the locations at which Books of Remembrance were available for signing. Some friends did go, and waited nearly ten hours to sign their names. When I asked them why they did this – the very idea struck me as odd, since their wait took place overnight and they had jobs to go to in the morning – they had no answer. Indeed, they are self-identified as being indifferent to the monarchy, and claimed they were not especially moved by Diana's death. They would not have said that they were grieving.

What struck me as strange was that in all the places I visited, other than the shopfront memorials, people went about their business normally. When I stopped in a café for coffee or lunch, the customers were talking, laughing, and carrying on the normal conversations one would expect, with no outward signs of any disruptions to their lives. The culmination of the week for me was leaving London for a brief holiday in Alsace on the Saturday morning of Diana's funeral. We had collected a hire car on the previous day, and drove immediately to Lichfield to leave our dog with my partner's parents for the time we would be away. We noticed that workers were tending to the verges on the M1 and assumed (correctly) that this must be in preparation for the funeral and the final journey to Althorp. When we returned to London late that afternoon, traffic was no greater than we might have expected on a Friday evening either going into or leaving London.

Because we expected large crowds coming into London for the funeral, we decided to leave our flat at 3:00 am. in order to avoid the traffic. In addition, we were covering a fair distance, travelling that day to Molsheim, near Strasbourg. In what was one of the bizarre coincidences from our standpoint, we had reservations in the Hotel

Diana, a booking which we had made some two months previously. That evening, we watched a repeat broadcast of the funeral on BBC; we could have watched it on German or French television, as the coverage seemed to be shared by all of the broadcasting outlets.

We drove through London first down Holloway Road, then through Upper Street in Islington, through the City and on to the Old Kent Road. We were struck by the numbers of people on the streets simply milling around. At first we thought they were early arrivals for the funeral, but we soon realised that they were people who were leaving different clubs along the route. Most of those we saw were in their twenties or thirties, of varying colours and genders, and many appeared to be either mildly intoxicated from alcohol or high on drugs. Most seemed to be enjoying themselves. Indeed, throughout our drive through London *en route* to the Channel Tunnel, the scene was much the same. Young and not-so-young people were engaged in a normal Friday night routine. They were behaving as if nothing of any consequence had occurred. The spaces they were occupying were fun spaces, not grieving and mourning spaces.

But how could this be? The newspapers were filled with stories of a nation in despair, a nation questioning itself and its values. People were introspective and angry with what they believed was the lack of any meaningful reaction by the Queen and other members of the Royal Family to the nation's loss. We watched as the Queen and others in the family returned to London ahead of the funeral, and saw the Queen address the nation. We were told the nation was angry and that as result the Royal Family would have to alter its ways of behaving. Yet against this backdrop, I had witnessed a normal London in which people behaved as they always did, with the obvious exceptions of the royal palaces and the areas immediately sur- rounding them. Only these public spaces seemed to contain the large numbers of people ostensibly mourning Diana.

As an American who experienced the period following the assas- sination of both Kennedy brothers and of Martin Luther King, I began thinking about the reactions of citizens particularly those which followed the death of John F Kennedy on 22 November 1963. Immediately following the announcement of his passing, I was driving my mother to work through Miami, Florida where we lived. We saw people standing still in the streets crying as, indeed, we ourselves were. In contrast, on the Sunday morning Diana died, my partner and I had breakfast in Highgate Village and were among dozens of people behaving no differently than they normally do. Following the Kennedy assassination of 1963, life in America came to a virtual halt until the funeral itself. Yet, in the week following Diana's death, no particular changes in the normal routines of life for citizens seem to have taken place. This may reflect the fact that Kennedy was Head of State; that would clearly make a difference. But what I am concerned with is the sense of loss people felt and how this could be observed in their outward behaviour .

Many studies have been made in the United States of the reaction to John Kennedys death. The speed with which the news spread is sometimes taken as quite astonishing – within five hours of his murder, 99.8% of the population knew of it.[1] But realistically, since the invention and popularisation of the broadcasting media, the widespread dissemination of news must be taken for granted, so the Kennedy figures ought not come as a great surprise. All that would now inhibit the spread of such news is the timing of the event, the location, and the speed with which those most intimately connected with it wished to make an announcement. The delay in news of Franklin Roosevelt's death on 12 April 1945, one of my earliest memories, is related to all these points.

But the whole process of grieving is another matter entirely. In the aftermath of John Kennedy's death, the Sheatsley and Feldman study, using a sample of 1400 adults interviewed within a week of the assassination, came to the following conclusions about how the respondents reacted:

– Preoccupation with the death was almost total;

– Nine out of ten people reported experiencing one or more of such physical symptoms as headache, upset stomach, tiredness, dizziness or loss of appetite;

– Two-thirds of respondents felt very tense and nervous during the four days;

– A majority of respondents confessed to feeling dazed and numb;

– Most people - men and women - cried at some period during this time;

– The event was compared most often to the death of a parent or close friend or relative;

– There was a tendency to react to the assassination in terms of personal grief and loss rather than in terms of anxiety for the future or of political or ideological concern.[2]

If we take all seven of these feelings which people expressed, we are looking largely at a sense of individual loss that any person might feel with the death of a loved one, a definition, as it were, of grief. Grief in almost all senses is a private feeling, a feeling which leads to the withdrawal from the world by those who have suffered a personal loss and which is accompanied by a degree of pain not normally felt. Mourning is the formalised behaviour that accompanies grieving. Because some people tend to be embarrassed by the grief of others, mourning in northern countries especially, as well as in the United States, has tended to be privately or quietly performed; there are a few notable exceptions as, for example, among the more outwardly emotional sections of the Afro-Caribbean community in Britain or the African American communities in the United States.

But in the United States, the dominant mode of private grieving and mourning seems to have followed Kennedy's assassination. Public events were cancelled in what is a busy time of year because of the Thanksgiving Holiday, many shops and businesses closed until after the funeral and people largely withdrew into their own homes to watch events surrounding the President's death on television. It was a surprisingly quiet period for a country in which citizens are reputed to be so expressive with their feelings. Of course, John Kennedy was assassinated in the early 1960s, before the decade we now remember as a kind of turning point in terms of modernity and what is now post-modernity. The rebelliousness of the 1960s followed the Kennedy assassination, it did not precede it, although its first glimmerings were apparent before then. However, the reaction to his death was typical of a family-centred, religious people for whom grief was still a private feeling and mourning was something to be carried out as discreetly and quietly as possible. What the response today would be is another matter entirely, but the context in which the murder of John Kennedy occurred was, I think, largely determinate of the type of response by American citizens, a response in which virtually the entire populated United States became a mourning area. Most people – though I would not claim that it was universal – were moved by his death and responded in a manner appropriate to the time and the culture.

Using the Kennedy assassination as a benchmark and point of

comparison, most public space, i.e., that space outside the private sphere in which grieving occurred, was mourning space. In the week which followed Diana's death, most public space was *not* mourning space. Indeed, very few spaces could be identified as areas of mourning. Those who wished to mourn gravitated to a few public spaces where people who had similar intentions went, too. Whether the move to a few public spaces, obvious ones given the royal connections, was exaggerated by news coverage, we cannot say, but the main concentration of that coverage was certainly centred there. But in general, most public spaces remained curiously ordinary as if nothing had actually happened. However, in the areas surrounding Buckingham Palace, Kensington Palace and St. James' Palace, large numbers of people gravitated ostensibly to mourn. This mourning was public and was open, but it was limited by space, something which had not occurred when Kennedy died. People went about their lives in a normal fashion in most of the country, When people 'chose' to 'mourn' they went to particular places to display feelings in a very public and obvious way, something which, it could be argued, is a departure from normal British behaviour.

At first, like most people watching television, listening to the radio or reading newspapers, I found the image of the masses mourning quite astonishing. The scenes around the palaces were, for lack of a better term, amazing, given the absence of obvious signs of mourning as reflecting grief elsewhere. This behaviour was totally unlike what occurred in the aftermath of John Kennedy's death. How may this be explained?

One explanation to which I have already alluded is the fact that President Kennedy was both the political and ceremonial Head of State; Diana did not fill either of these roles. Her involvement with issues of a political nature may have been a factor in measuring the interest the public had in her but, that is speculation. Another explanation widely heard is that she had become a kind of icon, widely photographed with her image staring out at people almost anywhere they happened to be in the public spaces they entered. This may have reflected the view that she was a very beautiful young woman, for certainly in the conventional sense the fact that she was considered to be beautiful can be taken as granted. But in that sense, there are many beautiful women in the public sphere who would not have elicited such a response. It could be that her celebrity was not based on her political role, such as it was, but was instead rooted in the idea the she had in some way suffered, considering the nature of her marriage, divorce and death. But perhaps this explanation makes her too reminiscent of Marilyn Monroe or Judy Garland, and the public reaction to their deaths, even in certain mourning spaces, was certainly more muted than the public mourning following Diana's. The death of Jacqueline Kennedy Onassis, widely reported and covered both in the United States and abroad, produced no such public movement to certain mourning spaces despite the coverage and widespread sadness surrounding her death.

Perhaps part of the explanation lies in the time Diana's death occurred. If we were to dissect the mass(es) who actually found their way to the particular public spaces in which mourning took place, we would probably find large numbers who were there out of curiosity. A large proportion may also have been foreigners – the day she died, 31 August, was at the end of the very busy summer period in which large numbers of foreign visitors are in London. I was struck at the time that those speaking with journalists were not all British – although this argument could also lay claim to the universality of Diana's appeal. And, of course, a large number of people may have felt a particular need to mourn with others, in public and away from what only could be termed 'normal' Britain, the space in which life went on as usual.

But if grief is a private emotion, i.e., what a person feels and how a death affects that person, and mourning is that activity which reflects that grief, then the public display we observed on television was quite different from what we normally expect from mourning. The movement to what became mourning areas was an extraordinary sight, but one which suggests to me that the private emotion of grief which would have led to a different type of mourning was largely absent. Indeed, it may be argued that widespread grief in Britain would have been accompanied by a withdrawal from normal life; the streets would have been quieter and the population more restrained.

Instead, for those so inclined mourning became a very public act removed from the constraints which normally are to be found among grieving people. In a curious way, the public display took over with the drift toward a few public spaces in order for people to mourn with others, but also for those who were there to demonstrate that they were, in fact, mourning. Compare this with the view of Geoffrey Gorer writing in 1965 that Britain was a society in which the 'majority wish to ignore grief and treat mourning as morbid'.[3]

Looked at in another way, people then would have been embarrassed by such public display. It would have been foreign to their nature. Most people when Gorer was writing would have thought of it as vulgar, some kind of performance and showing off, rather than true mourning.

Of course, we are more than thirty years beyond that. For some – indeed, for many if we accept the views of the tabloid press – the very absence of public display might be seen now as an absence of feeling, an absence of grief. Indeed, much of the criticism of the Royal Family suggests that public display of mourning is now expected, at least by many who help form and shape public opinion. For the Royal Family, Gorer's description of how the British once looked at grief and mourning is the model to be observed. But now we live in an era in which even men may cry, and cry publicly at that. Not to do so suggests an absence of feeling.

From my own perspective, the overt displays we witnessed are still an exception and not yet the norm. Most people went about their regular lives, did not break from their normal routines and did not attend the public spaces where mourning was not, I think, so much a reflection of grief as the behaviour of people who thought such actions appropriate. It may be argued that had this been a grieving nation, mourning spaces would not have been needed; all of Britain would have been mourning space as was the United States after John Kennedy's death.

In the end, Diana's death may well have been the occasion of sadness on the part of large numbers of people. One would have expected this to be the reaction of most people in Britain and elsewhere. She was after all a young woman who had so much ahead of her, perhaps an entirely new life which would be more private and normal. Thirty-six years is too short a life, only half the biblical span. But the response of the British public, not only those who attended the mourning spaces, represented a different kind of reaction than collective grief. Diana's space was a 'created' space largely because most of the country was not a mourning space – people in the main were not grieving for her in the way that term may be understood as it applies to Britain. But Diana's mourning space did provide room for a type of public display perhaps unique in modern British history, for those who wanted to act in a way which seemed appropriate to them even if it ran counter to longstanding traditions. But I would argue that what we observed was not the reflex of a grieving people, but rather that of a small part of the population who, in the more expressive 1990s, believe the absence of display is the absence of feeling. And in these touchy-feely days, expressive feeling, particularly in the presence of others, is the only real emotion worthy of the name for an increasing number. But to express such feelings, a public space must be created and this, I think, is the main legacy of the spatial Diana – for if the recent surveys are anything to go by, precious little else remains of that extraordinary week.

## References

1  Paul B. Sheatsley and Jacob J. Feldman, 'The Assassination of President Kennedy: A Preliminary Report on Public Reactions and Behaviour', from Robert Evans (ed.), *Readings in Collective Behaviour*, Chicago, Rand McNally & Co, 1969, pp. 259-283, p. 262.
2  Glenn M. Vernon, *Sociology and Death: An Analysis of Death-Related Behaviour*, New York, The Ronald Press Co., 1970, p. 149.
3  Glenn M. Vernon, *Sociology and Death*, p. 143. 1 2 3 204

# Index